START
SCALE
SELL

75 LESSONS FOR
BUSINESS SUCCESS

NICK SUCKLEY

First published in Great Britain by Practical Inspiration Publishing, 2020

© Nick Suckley, 2020

The moral rights of the author have been asserted

ISBN 9781788601832 (print)
9781788601856 (epub)
9781788601849 (mobi)

Every effort has been made to trace copyright holders and to obtain their permission for the use of copyright material. The publisher apologizes for any errors or omissions and would be grateful if notified of any corrections that should be incorporated in future reprints or editions of this book.

Practical Inspiration
PUBLISHING

MIX
Paper from
responsible sources
FSC® C013604

Contents

About the author

Over a 20-year period, Nick has launched and sold four companies. His first company sold within 18 months and his latest sold for £12m.

Nick started his career in advertising, working for agencies like Redheads, McCann-Erickson and MediaCom as well as a stint at the *Daily Express*. In the mid-1990s he was one of the people who saw the early potential for the internet and its role as an advertising platform.

In 1998, with long-term business partner, Pete Robins, and Rick Sareen, he launched Media21, one of the UK's first digital media agencies, and sold it to Grey London at the height of the dot-com boom just 18 months after its formation. The dot-com crash that followed shortly after was tricky, to put it mildly, but he survived to tell the tale.

Nick was also a founding investor in digital creative hot shop, Glue London (which sold to Aegis Group in 2005 for £14m) and launched and incubated DataShaka, an analytics software business where he was instrumental in securing several rounds of venture capital funding from Seedcloud Ventures.

Agenda21, the multi-award-winning digital media consultancy he set up with Pete Robins and Rhys Williams, was sold to Be Heard Group Plc for £12m in 2015.

Nowadays, Nick is a much sought-after consultant for media and technology entrepreneurs and C-level executives, advising them on opportunistic corporate build strategies and how to avoid the costly mistakes frequently associated with rapid growth and a changing marketplace.

Preface: lessons learned

Over the last 20 years I've seen lots of companies facing the same issues and lots of companies making the same mistakes, falling into the same traps that can be growth limiting or even terminal. There are many common causes of failure in the early days and many things that can hold back business growth in more mature companies. And there is a definite life-cycle that companies grow through on their way to maturity.

There are many inspirational books by self-made people talking about their success, but very few books seem to offer *practical* help with starting or growing or selling a business.

Hopefully this book will deliver that. I've grown and sold businesses a number of times and I've got the battle scars to show for it. In my view, if you can remove common problems, you're more likely to be left with a successful business. Or at least a business that will be more successful than it would otherwise have been. Even if you only apply one or two of the lessons learned in this book (and I hope more than one or two are useful) then it will more than cover the price of the book.

Here are just some of the lessons that I've learned along the way and now want to share with you:

- Why you should build a Founder's Mindset before you even start – something I've been doing for over 20 years (Lesson 1)
- Why the six-month effect can ruin your planning – far enough away for optimism to kick in but near enough to be dangerous (Lesson 5)

- The importance of just getting up and doing it – the most unsuccessful business never gets started (Lesson 16)
- Why everyone needs an elevator pitch (Lesson 32)
- Why getting the right management information will help you make the right decisions (Lesson 34)
- My favourite lesson of all, my Golden Rule for making profits (Lesson 38)
- Why the Power of Three will help you remain focused (Lesson 48)
- And lastly, the important lesson of thinking about what happens after you sell your business – this is the one that catches so many people out (Lesson 75).

Some of lessons in the book may seem obvious. But knowing the theory doesn't always mean putting that theory into practice is easy. *Start. Scale. Sell* offers bite-sized, no-nonsense and, most of all, *practical* lessons for even the most time-poor entrepreneur.

I've made plenty of mistakes over the years so I hope what follows will give you a head start – that you'll benefit from the lessons I've learned the hard way.

Nick Suckley

January 2020

Postscript 2020: A note on Covid-19

We were putting this book to bed just as the Covid-19 virus was taking hold and the UK was heading into lockdown. Who would have thought, even a month ago, that this virus would have such a rapid and deep impact on our economy?

It just goes to show that just like the recession of the early 1990s, the Dot Com crash of 2000 and the Credit Crunch of 2008, it is impossible to predict the nature of the next downturn.

Whatever downturn comes, some things never change – poorly run companies with excessive debt will be exposed and will most likely fail. What you can do is ensure your business is in the best shape it can be to survive and come out the other side thriving.

Looking back over my book, the lessons in the "Surviving Tough Times" section are all the more relevant and I would not change any of them. In particular:

Lesson 6 – I suspect many companies with excessive debt will fail during the lockdown. If they do survive they may struggle to capitalise on the rebound that is likely to happen at the end of this crisis.

Lesson 23 – Having a war chest of 6 months is always a good idea. It could be the difference between failure or survival.

Lesson 38 – The Golden Rule applies on the downside too. If your income is falling then your costs need to follow suit. That said, government support to furlough people means that redundancies are not inevitable. Resource, and more importantly skills and goodwill, will be retained in businesses to deal with the recovery.

Well-run and well-differentiated companies will be far better placed to weather the storm so make sure yours is one of them. I don't know what kind of country and economy we will be on the other side but I do know that getting the basics right will keep you in as strong a position as possible.

And don't forget that companies as diverse as Salesforce, Microsoft, Uber and AirBnB all launched during downturns. Societies change during a downturn and new opportunities can arise so now might be a good time to start something too!

Good luck!

Acknowledgements

This book began with a conversation with Jonny Wilks, who was an ex-client of mine from Investec Bank. Our friendship started with us talking about starting businesses – something Jonny was really keen to do. He urged me to write it all down so that he could buy and read it. I'd never have thought that the things I'd done would be worthy of consumption by others but as I was in my non-compete period from Agenda21 I was at a bit of a loose end.

I knew that once I began writing I would see the project through. I was hugely reluctant to start the task because of that. I didn't quite know what was involved in writing a book (or whether getting something published was even realistic) but I knew that it would be time-consuming.

Nevertheless I did start writing and in an early conversation with Richard Edwards (who runs our tech company DataShaka) one of the key features of the book emerged – the idea of teasing out the lessons learned.

Another critical conversation was with Sam Bowen, who ran a PR company that I was involved with. Aside from his support more generally, he was able to articulate what was relevant to readers about my background and achievements. By nature, I'm not at all showy and tend to underplay things and this means that I'm often guilty of underselling myself – especially when compared to many of the self-styled business experts who seem to inhabit places like LinkedIn. Sam was able to help me tease out what I call the "so what" in what I've done without it sounding undignified.

When I had finished my first draft I was introduced to Clare Grist Taylor, who is an agent and editor. Her feedback that my first draft was too much about the ad industry to be relevant meant a complete re-write, and with her help I focused even more clearly on the lessons learned. Her way with words made me realize that some people can write and some people can't!

Thank you all for helping me to produce something that I'm proud of and that I hope people will enjoy and benefit from.

And of course, a huge thank you to Kathrin, my wife, who has cheered me on from the sidelines throughout my career and has been a constant source of support while I've been working on this book. A number of times I caught her laughing while reading my first (more autobiographical) draft on her Kindle. "It's not supposed to be funny," I said. "It's not funny," she replied. "It's just that I remember everything that happened, just from an outside perspective. It's fascinating to read about it all again."

START

Chapter 1

Lessons for how to get started

Lots of people think about starting a business or company. Some do it – but, in the UK, 20% of new businesses fail in their first year and only around half will survive until their third year. I see a lot of common factors that cause young businesses to fail and I see a lot of common factors that hold rapidly growing businesses back from achieving their fullest potential. So how do you ensure success? In this section I explore the kinds of issues that founders are likely to encounter in the early days: why getting into your Founder's Mindset is so important; why you need to understand how much demand there is for your product or service; why a well-thought-out business plan is not just a piece of boring admin standing between your idea and endless riches; how to plan; how hard to work; and how to raise external finance.

The lessons in this chapter give your business a fighting chance of success and I mean this in the wider context – there is no point having business success if you hate your life. It is also crucial to look after yourself and ensure the business works for you and not the other way around.

Lesson 1: The Founder's Mindset. Treat yourself as self-employed even if you have a job

I have often asked myself the question of how I got started. Funnily enough, I developed a start-up mindset long before I actually started my first business. My father ran his own painting and decorating company and his advice is what really got me going: even if you have a job, think of yourself as being self-employed – you will be in a better position than most by thinking about running a business and starting to gather the funds to start up while you're still employed.

First, what I earn and what I pay myself are different amounts. Why is this important? It separates your earnings from your income – an important distinction when running a company. Getting this mindset right is crucial, as it means the surplus can be used to do other things – even if it is just saved to be spent later. I call this is **The Founder's Mindset**.

Second, if you spend less than you earn, you are building up a financial war chest. As with any company, a war chest will help you weather an unexpected storm. From my point of view, it gave me the knowledge that I could walk away from my job if I needed to. That feeling of independence is critical; often the biggest thing holding people back from starting a business is the fear of losing out on a regular income. Remove that fear and you're far more likely to do what others only talk about. Break the cycle of being stuck as an employee by paying yourself less than you earn.

Lesson 2: It's all about spotting the opportunity. Is there a market for what you are doing?

New opportunities will come from the unlikeliest of places. It took three eureka moments to get me to my first idea. The trick isn't necessarily in taking advantage of them; it's actually spotting them in the first place. How do you attune your senses to spot them? Or is it more a question of pursuing a number of interesting opportunities in the knowledge that some will work and some will fail? And of course, the most obvious failure is the company that stays on the drawing board and never gets going.

My first eureka moment came a few years after graduating. I was working in an advertising agency media department, the part that decides where ads run (eg on TV or in newspapers).

One afternoon is etched in my mind. I saw two colleagues looking intently at a PC screen and went over and asked what was going on. Right there and then, I got my first glimpse of the thing called the internet. What I saw (and can still remember) was a very beige computer and some very pixelated text and a low-resolution logo for a US bank. As eureka moments go it was not that earth-shattering, but I did walk away knowing that I had just seen something really important. I might not have realized precisely why, but there was definitely something there.

A few weeks later, I was meeting with a client, and a consultant I had not met before entered the room. He was there to give the client some food for thought about what this thing called the internet could do for their marketing. I was a bystander, but I came away from the meeting thinking, "I could do that." There was nothing especially ground-breaking in what was being said, other than it was being talked about by people other than me.

That evening, my second eureka moment came as I was walking down the office steps onto a rainy and dark London street to get the Tube home. I saw the consultant leaving the car park in a Mercedes. At that point the penny dropped. "I'm doing that," I thought to myself. "That's what I want to do."

Although I didn't realize it then, when I look back, that was the first time I was able to spot an opportunity. At the time, I was simply interested in something that was new but it was definitely a turning point: I had realized that the internet would be important in the context of the work I was doing. And the thing that hit me the most was that nobody else seemed to be that interested. Maybe that's the biggest opportunity of all: seeing something that others miss.

Lesson 3: Don't underestimate how long it will take. Use the time from idea to execution wisely

The time between having the idea and putting the business into practice is going to be a longer slog than you realize. Raw enthusiasm is great and the temptation to just get started is overwhelming, but they're likely to result in premature failure. The successful start-ups I've seen use the time in between "I've got a great idea" and "this is how I'm going to put it into practice" to plan carefully and properly, focusing on operational detail and taking into account the possible need to self-fund if business is slower to arrive than expected.

That's why having a proper business plan is so important, not just because your investors need it, but because it forces you to slow down and think about all the possible risks and how to prepare for or mitigate them. I slowed myself down by getting another job to gain more experience.

After looking at several opportunities, I accepted a job in the strategic planning team at the *Daily Express*. The team's aim was to pull together more "interesting" packages of advertising from the range of *Express* brands.

Moving jobs for money is rarely a good idea, and even on the first day I realized I would not be there for the long term, but it did provide more experience that I could draw on when launching my own business. I really didn't enjoy working at the *Express*, but it did get me going – and I got some great exposure to the advertising potential of the internet.

I had my third eureka moment on a train, when the idea for an internet advertising agency hit me. I can still feel the flash of realization 20 years on. It really was like a flicking a light switch. In fact, it seemed so obvious that I could not believe that others hadn't had the same idea already. I really wanted to get motoring.

I can't overstate how big a change this internet thing was. Nowadays, it's all taken for granted, but, then, it represented a seismic shift. I had a real sense of coming change. What was striking was that most of the large advertising agencies were not interested in it. At best it was a sideline; at worst it was being ignored.

Advertisers may have been interested in the internet, but agencies weren't delivering. This created a vacuum that was filled by the web agencies like the UK's Webmedia. But they mainly built websites. My thinking was those websites would need traffic; otherwise no one would know they were there. There must be demand for an agency that would replace the kind of work I'd been doing, just online. This was supported by what I saw in the *Daily Express* online sales team. They were selling internet advertising banners, but not to agencies. It was advertisers themselves that were booking their own ad slots. A particular standout was Eidos spending a lot of money on MegaStar to support the launch of their new game, Tomb Raider. No agency involved at all.

I was going to start an agency for the internet age.

Lesson 4: Take time with your business plan. You won't think of everything but it will help

The Advertising Director at the *Express* was a really nice guy but he had a way of walking around the sales floor that reminded me of a ferocious beast prowling his territory. There were times when I seriously thought I could see this guy hitting someone. Sometime later, at our annual sales conference, I asked what the prowling was all about. He said, "Walk slowly, Nick. You'll be amazed what you find out." I try whenever I can to walk slowly around my people. It's amazing what you can pick up and how you can spot and avoid problems before they get worse.

What I found as I walked around was that, for advertisers, the internet meant building websites. Websites were built but then nobody would visit, because there was no way of finding them. Surely there was a business in this. Why would you go to the trouble and expense of building a website and then not tell anyone about it?

For me, the idea wouldn't go away, so I decided to act on it and I began the process of starting a business. In the late 1990s there was nothing like the kind of help that exists now, like business incubators (places where you can hone your business idea) and business accelerators (where you can take your idea and build the business case to show that it is investable), both amazing resources that can help you get going. I was going to have to do it the hard way.

I wrote a business plan with a profit and loss (P&L) and a cashflow based on a purely theoretical set of clients and realized that the cashflow element of my business would be tricky unless managed well. This is the one element that has never changed; the old cliché that cash is king really is true. My problem was that, in buying media, you're likely to have to pay the media supplier for the ad space before the client has paid you – problematic for a small company with limited resources. I would need to find a way to get around this. My market research consisted of talking to advertisers while at the *Express*, and taking note of what I saw around me.

I could not wait to get started, but there was a lot to be done before I could begin, not least saving up the money I'd have to live on until the business got going. It took almost a year between making the decision and actually leaving the *Express*. The frustration was huge as I was ready to go right now. Surely advertisers would be desperate to buy my services. All I'd have to do was call them up and money would start flowing.

During that frustrating year, I attended a start-up course with a mixture of people with a range of business ideas. Mine, of course, was different: I was going to take over the world with internet advertising. Every single person in the room had more enthusiasm than they had done planning. Everyone in the room was ready to go *right now*. In actual fact, most of the other attendees were making critical mistakes: jumping in without planning, relying on raw enthusiasm, impatient to get started. Looking back, that kind of enthusiasm is crucial but, unless you're incredibly lucky, you also need to plan for the setbacks, the failures and the trip-ups. Failing to prepare really is preparing to fail.

A business plan isn't a piece of bureaucracy standing between you and success. It forces you to really understand your market, where demand really lies and how you can compete. It will also help you to unearth risk factors you may have overlooked. Practical mistakes are likely to be more expensive than theoretical ones in your business plan.

Lesson 5: The Six-Month Effect. Hope for the best and plan for the worst

What is the worst that can happen if I start up? This is where my wife Kathrin came in. She always has an eye on the practicalities of a decision. Usually it involves her asking: "What if it fails or doesn't work out. What happens then?"

For my first business, that calculation was straightforward: if it works, then great. If it fails, I go back and get another job. Therefore, I had nothing to lose by trying. I estimated that it would be six months before any income would come in – a purely made-up time span I now call **The Six-Month Effect**. I thought that six months sounded far enough away for things to start happening, but soon enough to be relevant to a business plan. I've found over the last 20 years that The Six-Month Effect can be really dangerous when planning for new income. It sounds credible, but it can create a false sense of positive change. I've learned always to be on the lookout for The Six-Month Effect – then double the time you'll need to get things off the ground, and quantify carefully the steps you'll need to take to meet carefully calibrated milestones. For example, if you need to win new customers, ask yourself exactly what you are doing to ensure you will win client X in X months. And be realistic: client X needs to be a named client you've already made contact with; otherwise it's pie in the sky.

It's better to err on the side of caution in the early days. Give yourself the time you need for the money to start coming in. Nothing is more frustrating than having to give up because you didn't plan for a long enough lead-in time.

This happened to a company I mentored. The founder had a brilliant idea for a tech business, but it took him longer to win customers than he expected. With a wife and young child, he only had a limited window and, in the end, he had to find a job to pay the bills. His backup plan was to run the business evenings and weekends but this was never really going to be feasible. He lost momentum and, busy in his day job, struggled to meet the prospective customers he needed. I suspect if he had had an extra few months' money to live on, things could have been very different. Great business idea, great timing and a huge amount of time invested, but the business failed because he had not planned for things taking longer than expected.

Lesson 6: Banks – beware

Don't rely on the high street banks if you can avoid it. They usually want to give you money when you don't need it, but, if you do need it, they won't be there. Work your plans so that you don't ever need to rely on them. At the very least, this removes one more unnecessary failure factor. Financing with bank debt can be a very bad option. You may not have to dilute your equity holding, but all sorts of external events can lead to them demanding their money back – just at the time when you most need it. During the credit crunch of 2008 there were numerous cases of solvent companies going to the wall because banks decided they needed their money back.

With my very first business my bank said they'd back me. With hindsight, that was laughable. What they really meant was they'd give me an overdraft facility equal to the amount of money I'd put in. The Six-Month Effect meant I planned I'd need about £3.5k to live on while I got started because my wife was working and could pay the rent and bills. I seriously underestimated how long it would take to start earning money.

With Agenda21, our bank branch on Soho Square were great. They were used by many agencies like us so they understood the kind of business we were. But it always felt like they were trying to sell us something – regardless of whether we needed it or not.

Loans to get you started and overdrafts to fund cashflow ups and downs are common uses of bank finance. The trouble is, though, as shown by the recent RBS small business scandal, where the bank forced businesses to close, the interests of a bank and your business can diverge quickly and fatally. Because of this, I'm not a fan of bank finance. There are many more equity finance options available, especially when interest rates are low. When you pair that up with investors who are used to dealing with early-stage companies, you're much less likely to have the rug pulled from beneath you.

Look out, too, for central and local government-backed schemes to help start-ups. Often these offer better terms than banks and may not require such onerous guarantees. There are many private grant initiatives that are worth hunting out too.

I'm also a fan of good old-fashioned saving up. Boot strapping is an option that may mean you grow slowly in the early years, but at least you'll avoid the pitfalls of relying on a bank. And, by not diluting ownership in return for funding, you'll own all of your company.

I suspect many companies with excessive debt will fail during the lockdown. If they do survive they may struggle to capitalise on the rebound that is likely to happen at the end of this crisis.

Lesson 7: Look after your business by looking after yourself

There is a reason why smarter investors want their founders to earn more than a bare-bones salary. And it's the same reason you need to allow yourself enough to do more than just exist. Setting up a business is an emotional slog, made worse if you have no money. Investors will view it as a risk to the business if you are reliant on an earning partner or you're lonely and miserable with no money. Either way, the risk that you could just pack it all in is high – and all for the sake of an extra couple of hundred pounds a month.

The date is etched into my brain: I'd resigned from the *Daily Express* and left just before the August Bank Holiday in 1998. I was full of optimism and I started work the following Tuesday on what was effectively a one-man business I called Suckley Media from our one-bedroom flat in west London.

Finding potential leads to talk to was difficult. Making them pay was even harder. The community centred around the trade magazine *New Media Age* was helpful – and confirmed my instinct that online advertising was going to be important – but it was so small that it often felt like an echo chamber.

Some people enjoy working from home but I hated it. Kathrin would leave for work and then I'd be left alone in our flat with a feeling of a mountain to climb, trying to create something from nothing.

My own lowest point came one day when I was hungry and went to the local Kwik Save. I had scraped together enough change to buy a jar of peanut butter. At the checkout, I put the jar in a carrier and the cashier asked for an extra 5p that I didn't have. I put the bag back and carried a lonely jar of peanut butter home on its own.

That's the point where I almost gave up. The thought of working in an office with fun colleagues and a regular salary was becoming ever more appealing. I gritted my teeth, put the thought out of my mind and kept going, but I also learned an important lesson about the false economy of not looking after yourself in the crucial early days.

One of the companies I mentor is in just that position. The founder thinks he's doing the right thing by taking a bare-bones salary. The reality is he's subsidizing the business and external investors' money and introducing an unnecessary risk. If he were to split up with his girlfriend (who is effectively funding him) or just get fed up of having no money, the whole business could fail. It is important to allow yourself a decent living for the tough journey ahead.

Lesson 8: How hard do I need to work? Have I earned my money today?

I call it **The Working from Home Paradox**. Working in a normal job involves all sorts of social interactions and interruptions, all of which distract you from the actual process of doing work. Working at home removes all of these distractions (and boy, did I miss them) and I was able to focus 100% on the job in hand. So, while I was able to cover a lot of ground on any given day, I struggled to know when to stop. The associated guilt that came with trying to get a business off the ground meant I was trying to stick to a full working day and I was feeling guilty when I wasn't. It was surprisingly tough, something I had simply not anticipated.

A friend of mine, Rick, who would eventually become a partner in that first company, Media21, had a great solution. "Have you earned your money today?" he said. His philosophy is that, on any given day, you need to earn your money for that day. Some days, that might mean just making the right three phone calls. On other days, you might have to work for hours. Sometimes, you may not even get to the point where you've earned your money. However, by focusing on quantifiable achievements, you're able to judge just how much work is enough. So, rather than saying "I've worked lots today", you can say "I've earned my money today" and stop.

I learned that it's important to chunk work down into component parts and focus on achievement rather than time spent working. On a good day, finish early: give yourself a break. On others, you may not get there, but don't beat yourself up too much. Focus on outcomes rather than the amount you've worked. For me, nothing is more satisfying than striking things off my to-do list. It helps me to judge how much is enough and offers a "reward" in the absence of anyone telling me what to do and when I've done well.

The cliché that building a business is a marathon and not a sprint really is true. Keep going day by day, pace yourself with daily, weekly and monthly objectives and give yourself a mechanism to know when to stop. There's no point burning yourself out and failing six months down the line.

Lesson 9: Push versus pull factors in getting started

Sometimes it's not just about spotting the opportunity; it's also about having sufficient push. As a first-time entrepreneur, I was drawn to starting something. The second time around, when Pete and I founded Agenda21, I had the added benefit of a push from a job I didn't like. For some people, losing your job can be just the trigger you need to get started. But you also need patience.

What is the push you need to get going? Deciding to do it is just the start. Having built and sold my first business, I knew how to build another one, but I needed a push to make it happen.

Back in 2005, Pete, my business partner, and I were working at MediaCom, one of the largest ad agencies in the world, who had bought our first company, Media21. We were frustrated at our inability to get MediaCom to do more to develop our digital offering, especially as we could see new developments coming in areas like mobile, email and ad technology.

In reality, a large company like MediaCom does not make its money by being a pioneer of new opportunities. Experimentation is expensive with no guarantee of commercial success. Pete and I were passionate about this new technology, getting in early and doing it for fun. In reality, they were frustrated with us and we were frustrated with them.

We agreed to wait until my daughter was a year old before we made the decision to resign. That gave us six months to plan out what our next venture should look like. Our reasoning was that there was risk in me being a new father; better to wait until things had settled down.

Change in digital is constant and our view was that advertisers were still poorly served by larger agencies. Funnily enough we were right back where we had started in 1998. Our fear had always been that large agencies would wake up to digital and steal our staff and clients. What we did not bargain on was the rate of digital change outstripping agencies' ability to deal with it. That was our sweet spot: an agency that would be agile enough to help clients plan campaigns to run in the best places.

We waited until 4 July 2005 – Independence Day – to resign. There was no particular reason for this date (it was Pete's idea) but it seemed like a good idea at the time. We were not planning to be bad leavers. We would work our notice and would not try to steal any MediaCom clients. It's doubtful whether any Medi-aCom clients would have wanted to go from the biggest agency in the UK to the smallest but I think MediaCom appreciated the sentiment.

We knew the continuing rate of tech change was an opportunity for us, and this time we had the experience to back it up. We just needed the push of being in the wrong jobs to make it happen, and the good sense to plan and time our departure properly.

Lesson 10: Get real about where your sales will come from

I see so many start-ups where the founders decided to manage their own sales process. I can understand why, but I think this is a mistake. For those of us from a non-sales background, it's not a core skill and often falls away when other work we prefer comes along. The sales pipeline inevitably suffers from not having someone dedicated to generating leads and potential sales. While the founders are the best people to articulate the company's purpose to clients, the rigour of making calls and generating contacts should not be underestimated.

On the day we moved into Agenda21's first offices, another recent start-up agency was moving out. One of their sales guys had been pursuing us for months. At the time, we just laughed at his persistence and lack of self-consciousness at pursuing another agency. When I look back now, it was a signal I missed, probably the most important decision I didn't take. It would be another seven years before we hired our first sales/

marketing person and I think our business was restricted as a consequence.

When it comes to sales, it's important to understand whether you're more naturally a "hunter", happy to be sales-focused, out there chasing business, or a "farmer", more suited to client or business management. Be honest with yourself: it's one of the most important things to recognize about how you need to grow your business. I'm a farmer and I can hunt pretty well. I also see many hunters who cannot farm. While not putting enough emphasis on having a dedicated "hunter" to focus on sales and marketing held us back, I've also seen businesses led by brilliant sales people who suffer from not being able to build client loyalty. The most successful businesses will do both well.

More natural farmers, like me, find it more difficult and stressful to hunt, so you need to think especially hard about where you are going to find your customers.

Lesson 11: Having little to lose in the early days means you can be ballsy. Don't underestimate the power of offering an outside view

With all of our clients in the early years of Agenda21, we were able to say to them: here's what you need to do to grow your business. We thought we were revolutionary in terms of doing digital media in a new way. The reality was we were simply doing it well. Everyone we worked with had similar challenges: they wanted to grow by getting more customers signed up. We were able to figure out where to run ads online to get people to click for as little money as possible.

What we actually had was a blunt focus on the commercials and no need to be polite – we were 100% focused on business, and customers appreciated it. I remember a meeting with UK Broadband's owner from Hong Kong where I pointed out that Direct Line took five steps to work out who you are and what your car is and give you a quote. In contrast, UK Broadband had seven steps just to sell someone broadband. They were asking for too much information and, with every unnecessary step, people give up. So, they were paying to get people onto their site only for them to leave halfway through signing up. "Oh," she said. "We hadn't thought of that."

Years earlier, during a pitch to the recently launched Egg credit card team I said, "You think you're a market leader producing advertising that looks like this" (ie not very good). My pitch was focused on showing them what I thought market-leading advertising looked like. We won the business.

Customers can often suffer from "group think" and often an outsider looking in can identify what is most important and what is not. The truth can be painful sometimes but many customers appreciate a ballsy opinion, provided it's well timed and delivered and helps them to improve.

Lesson 12: Making money while you sleep

I see the lesson I learned the hard way about the false economy of bare-bones founder salaries (see Lesson 7) replicated in almost every start-up I've worked with since. The desire to help the business get started by taking low (or zero) pay is worthy, but slogging away growing a business and not even budgeting for a pint or two at the end of the week is unrealistic. A demotivated founder, stuck in a role with no money to let off steam outside of work, is as risky to a new business as an unrealistic six-month horizon.

Agenda21's early days were pretty much hand to mouth. It dawned on me one day that when the business (Pete, myself and our third founder, Rhys) were not in the office, no work was being done. A successful business should make you money while you sleep. After six months, we had enough business and confidence to hire our first employee. It was not that we were too busy, but we needed the space to be on call and available for our clients. Too many businesses wait too long and get trapped into being too busy to take a step back and hire in the right support. It was still all hands on deck with four of us squeezed into a three-person office, but we'd made the first important step which allowed us to delegate and share the workload – and potential – of a growing company. We were ready to start making money while we slept.

Lesson 13: Raising external investment: beware the pitfalls

With the exception of ad tech company DataShaka, my companies have scaled up with minimal external investment. Agenda21, for example, started with me living off my own money for six months, effectively as an "investment" until business income started to flow.

For many companies, raising money feels like the right thing to do and may even feel quite clever. However, I see many founders ending up on the fundraising "conveyor belt" where they spend a large amount of their time either raising finance or trying to hit targets in order to raise the next round of funding before they run out of cash. While some capital-intensive businesses need to scale quickly, it is also worth bearing in mind that you can only sell shares in your company in return for investment once. Diluting ownership might be an attractive short-term funding option, but the downside is that you may end up owning a significantly smaller share of your company so that, even when the company is worth significantly more, your overall worth is unchanged.

By all means raise from friends and family, but I think it's usually better to own more of a company than less. Founder dilution was a big problem for a company I worked with recently. Subsequent rounds of finance meant the founders held only a small percentage of shares and I really did wonder why they continued to stick around. They had all the downsides of being a founder, the stress and worry, without the upside of a decent payout in the future.

Formal fundraising, let's call it a seed funding round, will never be the last round of funding you will need. Focusing on securing successive rounds of external funding can set in train a series of events over which you have little control – and could ultimately end up with you owning a vanishingly small stake in your own business. Some investors recognize the need to keep founders motivated, but many do not. Go into this process with your eyes open. Raising money can feel clever. Dilution to oblivion is less so. And don't forget the opportunity cost of time spent raising money and dealing with investors. Think about the dilemma encapsulated in the adage: when I'm running my business, I should be raising money and, when I'm raising money, I should be running my business.

I work with a technology business that's doing really well but the founder spends a huge amount of time moving from closing the last investment round to thinking about the next one. In his case, external investment really was the best option to help him scale up, but it is a distraction. An important distraction, but a distraction all the same.

Lesson 14: Company valuations: getting to your first £1m – and beyond

There are no hard and fast rules around how to value your business for the purposes of external investment. Market factors can vary widely between industries and sectors and will have an impact on how potential investors will value your business. That said, arriving at valuations for early-stage companies can be very subjective. So why not take the initiative and decide first? I often use the following points to reach an early valuation. Having as many as possible of these points worked out in detail will allow you to justify a higher valuation.

Going in to meet a potential investor with a clear idea of what your business is worth (provided it is realistic) is a sign of a leadership team who know where their business is going. This gives investors confidence.

Most companies with a decent business plan that has the following covered should be able to justify a valuation of £500k:

- a well-researched proposition in a market
- a market that is growing
- all the relevant government and tax approvals (eg in the UK HMRC approvals: SEIS or EIS)

- a clear idea of how the business will make money
- a clear idea of how the business will market itself and reach potential customers.

I would consider this a base-line valuation for a solid business plan. Being blunt, if you don't have these things covered off, your business isn't investable.

One you have this baseline, you can build other things into your valuation. For example:

- A working prototype or minimum viable product (MVP) that is already being used by a customer shows your potential for earning revenue from your product. A proof of concept (POC) with a customer will add to your valuation further.
- If you are already making money, even if it is below what you ultimately hope to charge, it shows an investor that you have a product that customers will pay for and that you already have an active sales and marketing effort.
- Patents or intellectual property (IP) unique to your company can push valuations even higher.

Investors love a company that has already done the hard work of building a product or service and has already secured revenue (repeat custom is even better). Where investment money is needed to help a company that is already up and running to scale up, investors can be reassured that many of the early-stage risks have been dealt with. Being able to demonstrate that your business is active as opposed to just being theoretical will help you to justify a higher (£1m) valuation.

Less tangibly, do not underestimate the following in building up your valuation:

- Your founding team has previous experience of your sector, or, even better, previously managed an exit previously in the sector.
- There is active investment or mergers and acquisitions (M&A) in the sector.
- Investor competition also helps.

Common watch-outs include things like poorly differentiated products or services and gaps in due diligence. And the biggest watch-out of all is a company that is missing a core team member or where there is a lack of buy-in from one or more key person. This can scare investors off altogether.

All of this only goes to show how subjective valuations can be. The trick is to build a case while identifying and eliminating as many risk factors as possible.

Chapter 2

Lessons for scale: the growth phase

At this stage of your company's development, you need to decide the kind of company you want to be: your purpose and values and what you are willing to put up with from customers. It is alignment time, too – time to get your shareholdings right and to understand how your company will make money. Cash really is king and you will need to hustle for growth.

It is also the time when the founders' roles may start to change. This is important, as it is the time when your company will have scaled to the point where it begins to be more like a machine. That means you need to understand how you can be as efficient as possible by establishing good business habits around growth and profitability. You may also have to start to delegate some business operations to others.

Lesson 15: Sweat equity: you can only sell shares in your company once, so be smart about how much you trade, and for what

Once sold (or given away in exchange), it's very difficult to buy shares back. As we saw in Lesson 13, there are no rights and wrongs here, but the temptation to give up shares in lieu of money in the early days can be overwhelming for cash-strapped start-ups. I've often seen situations where tech start-ups trade a significant share of their business to an outsourced tech company to "fund" their prototype. Trading equity for work can be a good idea; just be aware of what you are giving away and make sure the deal is worthwhile – not just for now but also in the years to come. Right now, your shares may be cheap but, in a few years' time, will you still be happy with a significant shareholder whose contribution was made years previously? More than anything, you really must make sure you value your business properly.

In early 1999, when we had started our first agency, Media21, I was introduced to a website design company called Deepend. It was run by three friends who had studied together at the Royal College of Art. They had recently moved into an old warehouse in Shoreditch, had more space than they could fill and were keen to fill it with like-minded companies. The warehouse was the epitome of cool: rubber floors, an aeroplane wing for the boardroom table and beanbags – all fairly normal now but new and distinctive 20 years ago.

We did a deal where Deepend would give us office space, back office help with finance, and reception and IT support. The cost to us was 4% of our company based on a £500k valuation – so £20k worth of value. It was an easy decision to make and we all agreed to go ahead. While the office space had a tangible cost and value to the business, it was the intangible value of Media21 getting up and running really quickly that was the most significant. The rub-off effect of being in such cool offices also helped us more than we realized when we did the deal. With hindsight, it was a really smart deal that paid back many times over.

This kind of equity for in-kind deal worked for us. It gave our start-up an instant kick-start and, in the end, 4% was not huge because we had valued our business properly. It was a good deal for both parties.

Removing the hassle of back office functions meant that we were up and running overnight; we were free to focus on the day job of winning business and growing the company.

Lesson 16: Just do it

Two things stand out about how we grew Media21.

When we moved into Deepend's offices, the effect of being in a proper office was transformative. Looking like an agency meant we behaved like one and customers thought we were more than a start-up that was a few weeks old.

Once we moved in, we spoke to anyone who would listen. We used the fact that regular agencies didn't get the internet and it was helpful to have an "enemy" we could push against. Coincidentally, there was huge demand from companies capitalizing on the dot-com boom and, in short order, we picked up many of the early dot-com advertisers, like UpMyStreet, Blue Square, QXL and BOL.com, an early rival bookseller to Amazon. Just being in the market meant we had clients knocking on our door. The market was so new that there were only a handful of companies working in our space – competition was not fierce.

The secret of our early success was simply that we did it. Where others talked, we started a business and shouted about it. At the height of the dot-com boom, that in itself was enough to scale up. Looking back, the only difference between us and others was that we *did* it rather than just *talking* about it. We did not have any unique talent or anything special to offer. We simply provided a service to customers who needed it. It may sound obvious, but starting a business where there is real demand is one of the surest ways of being successful.

Lesson 17: Walk the walk #1: establish your company values

Once, we had a bizarre meeting with an early online gaming website. During the meeting their MD behaved very oddly, walking in and out of the room while we were presenting. It was clear he was totally disinterested. We finished the meeting and walked back to our office, deciding on the way that we didn't want to work with them: if that was the way the company behaved then we were not interested – life is too short. When we told the MD, he was indignant that we didn't want to work with "the largest gaming site in the UK". We explained that we didn't choose our clients based on size. Shared values and culture were much more important to us.

We also got a call from an early music platform where musicians could use the site to self-publish. Their marketing director had previously worked for a big household name and asked if we wanted to meet up. It turned out he had already been talking to our main competitor, I-Level, and we soon realized that he was only using us to try to knock down I-Level's pricing. The temptation to try to win the business by undercutting I-Level was there but, deep down, we knew it was not right and, in all likelihood, they would not have worked with us anyway – even if we had been cheaper.

A principle is not a principle unless it costs you money. We had not set out to build a business with any kind of ethical principles, but we did take the view that if we had taken the risk of starting our own company, we were only going to work with people we wanted to work with and with whom we felt an affinity or "fit".

Lesson 18: Walk the walk #2: decide what you will stand for

In 2010, we began a relationship with a well-known printer company and so started what can only be described as a long-term love/hate relationship.

Our early meetings developed into what I called "ambush" meetings. Despite our best efforts, we would arrive for a meeting only to have the purpose of the meeting change. New people would appear, people would dial in from Germany, other agencies would be present. This chaos continued. While this was seemingly normal behaviour for our client, I was getting really fed up with it.

Slowly, however, we began to understand what was going on. The UK and German teams were competing to dominate marketing in Europe. There was also competition for control over the company's digital marketing. We realized halfway through one meeting that much of the work we were being asked to do was for an *internal* pitch. That explained the chaos and, once we realized it, we were able to better anticipate what we needed to do (and usually it was not what we'd been asked to do).

After that, we were able to tailor what we offered so that it made sense in their context, using simple and visual presentations that would go around the business and in particular to Japanese decision makers, too, who would not understand our usual pitch. It was far from our normal way of working, but it made us realize that hustling based on our own principles would only get us so far. Having principles is important, but so is understanding what your customers really need. Growing up, what we learned from working with this client formed the basis of how we would operate as a business. Our stated aim was to build long-term sustainable relationships with clients. We would invest heavily in our clients and do the very best work we could. Many years later, one of our contacts said Agenda21 was so trusted because not once did we ever let them down.

Lesson 19: Get your shareholdings right and adjust them if need be. It will avoid more serious problems down the line

When the three of us started Media21, the plan was that Pete and I would be running clients and going out and winning business. As a team we worked together really well. Pete came from a direct response media background and I was more brand-focused. Rick was what we called an "agency suit", meaning he was very skilled with people and making sure everyone was doing what they were supposed to be doing. The original plan was that he would spend a day or two a week with us helping out. Very quickly, the reality was that he was a full-time member and very much part of the business. His experience was invaluable and Pete and I agreed that we should equalize his shareholding to reflect his equal contribution to the business. We would all adjust so that we each owned 30% of Media21. We didn't have to do that and we could have kept a larger share for ourselves but, in equalizing things, we removed a huge potential for resentment. When things are running well, resentments don't surface, but, when things get tricky, you really want everyone pulling in the same direction to move the business on.

Later on, with Agenda21, we encountered a similar situation when Rhys joined our new start-up. He was a level below Pete and me and had less experience. We had no doubt he would be an invaluable member of the new team so we decided that Rhys should come in as an equal partner. I suspect he would have joined us even with a lower shareholding, but our thinking, again, was to counter potential long-term resentment. When you are in scale-up phase, being aligned and equally motivated is vitally important. Tensions are distracting and distraction is a risk that should be avoided at all costs.

Dysfunction in leadership teams can often be traced back to these kinds of inequalities. It is important to de-risk as much as possible. When things get tough a minority shareholder could easily wonder why they are working as hard as you when they own less of the company. Removing this barrier really did boost trust and meant we were all focused on the task of growing the business.

Lesson 20: Understand how you make money. Get your finances in order

Running Media21, a 10-person company with Deepend providing back office support, was pretty straightforward. In fact, it didn't feel that much different to working in any other agency job. Our process was straightforward: pitch some business, win it, find some people to work on it and repeat. Because we were all sitting together it was easy to keep tabs on what was happening and help out where needed. Managing the team by osmosis is easy when you're 10 people, not at all workable when you're 50 people and impossible by the time you hit 100. The most important thing is to understand how you make money. That may be stating the obvious, but companies really do only exist to make money and I am amazed how many companies don't seem to have this front of mind across all areas of the business.

How we made money was like this. In a campaign costing £100k, we would invoice the client for £100k but we would expect to receive invoices from suppliers of £85k. Each media owner supplier would offer us a 15% agency discount and that's where we made our money. The more campaigns we could run, the more commissions we would make and the more people we would need.

The only glitch we hit was around accounting. As part of our deal, we had access to Deepend's bookkeeper but she hadn't worked with a media agency before and it took her a while to recognize which elements of a media campaign were income and commission and which bits were due to be paid out to media owners when their bill landed.

It would often take months for media suppliers to send us an invoice and sometimes we never received one, meaning at any one time we'd have a number of campaigns that were still "open". We'd taken our 15% into income but the rest – the lion's share – was sloshing around waiting to be accounted for. It was here that I first encountered the most dangerous word in accounting – accruals. It sounds like a proper thing in accounting terms but I came to realize how much trouble it could cause. Because the bookkeeper didn't really understand the whole process and I didn't know the right questions to ask, accruals came to mean "I didn't know what to do with this money so I put it in accruals so that things would balance out." At Media21 our accrual pot was growing and it meant there was a risk we would spend money we didn't really own if (and when) suppliers eventually got around to invoicing us.

I am always amazed at how many people give so little thought to how the company makes and manages its money (or even an interest in whether the company made money at all). This really came to the fore when the dot-com bubble burst and we had some major decisions to make a year or so later. Get your finances right early. And if your accruals figure is larger than, say, a few thousand pounds, then you've got a problem. Deal with it early.

Lesson 21: Why productivity matters

Technology really can reduce costs and make people more efficient. Managers will always complain about needing to hire more people, but I prefer to look at ways to automate.

One day, Rick saw a couple of Deepend people heading down to the basement with a brand-new digital camera, a white sheet and a desk lamp. It turns out they were going to do what's known in the business as a packshot: photos of a physical product to be used on a website – in this case a vodka brand. It was shot on site in about 20 minutes. Rick asked how much they were charging the client for the work and they said about £60. Rick was dumbfounded; most agencies would charge thousands for the same thing. The end result was indistinguishable from something that would have taken an agency a whole day. What stays with me was Rick's view that he had seen the future and that it didn't bode well for creative agencies. Sitting here today, I'm pleased to say that creative agencies are still very much alive, but there is no doubt that the nature of the business has changed completely. What we were seeing at Deepend was the early disrupting effect of digital technology, allowing ordinary people to create quickly and cheaply.

More recently I've used technology to double digital profits at Goodstuff. The digital team I inherited were able to work on around £10m of business in the year I arrived. A number of technologies have helped the team work more effectively: for example, we automated the manual processes involved in running campaigns. A year later, the same team brought in £20m, just by being more productive. That's a huge amount of extra money earned with no extra costs.

I'm not suggesting that every company has a problem that can be so easily fixed with such big results, but even small gains are worthwhile. Productivity gains provide you with growth without having to find any new clients or make more sales. And, in the early days, the extra cash can fuel more growth – without the need for more external investment.

Lesson 22: Manage your cash as if your life depends on it

In the early days of any company, cashflow is critical. I cannot overstate its importance. At Media21, we mitigated some cash requirements with the deal with Deepend where we traded 4% of Media21 in exchange for rent and back office support (see

Lesson 15). It meant we only had to find cash to cover our own salaries, and had minimal outlay on other overheads. Not that we were complacent – no cash meant no pay. It's funny how, when you really need to earn money, you develop an edge – not desperation, more like hunger, and that hunger is positive and it shows how keen you are to work with customers. That can be appealing to customers who appreciate keenness.

We had a fairly basic process for managing the money: I ran a profit and loss spreadsheet (showing when income was billed or expenditure committed) and a cashflow spreadsheet (showing when the money actually arrived in or left our bank account). In the early days they might be much the same thing. But the key thing is to monitor regularly when you get paid and when you have to pay out.

When we launched Agenda21, getting cash to flow to all the moving parts when no one was willing to offer credit to such a young company was tricky. Cashflow became a major priority. Having escaped an agency environment, we were feisty and full of attitude at our new-found independence. I was happy to say to prospective clients that we were not a bank. Agenda21 did not exist to support its clients' cashflow and therefore we would need the money for ad campaigns upfront before we could commit to booking activity. Equally, I was very happy to offer credit of, say, 30 days on our fees or commission. Rather than take the risk to the business of even just one client defaulting on a campaign, which would leave Agenda21 on the hook for thousands we simply could not afford, we needed the cash in advance.

Surprisingly, most clients were happy with the arrangement. We would send an invoice (my favourite job in the whole world) and a few days later the money would land. The offer of credit on our fees was usually ignored as it was easier for them to process everything in one go.

I learned that there is no need to accept conventional wisdom on payment. I was surprised that our clients agreed without more of a fight, but it was necessary and we really were offering something different and new. The involvement of me or Pete or Rhys in their business was a big benefit and paying upfront was a trade-off they felt was worth making.

It was a good habit that persisted all the way through Agenda21's life. When we came to sell 10 years later, it made a massive difference to the working capital we could show on our balance sheet.

Lesson 23: Why every company needs a war chest

I have always used the default media banking option of Barclays in Soho Square, bankers to a number of media agencies. Before the days of internet banking, campaign money would be paid into our account and then we would need to pay suppliers for campaigns to go live. This involved filling out a paper form, acquiring two signatures and hand-delivering it to Barclays. I've lost count of the number of times we had to walk down to Soho Square, forms in hand, to get the money where it needed to go just to get our campaigns live.

Agenda21's big cash break came from ad agency Saatchi & Saatchi. Toshiba was one of their clients and they were about to launch HD DVD as a rival to Sony's Blu Ray. We developed a brilliant campaign that showcased HD DVD video by "sniffing out" the maximum resolution video someone could get based on their bandwidth to give people the best HD experience without annoying them. We ran the campaign with Yahoo across Europe, subsidized by Intel. It was a big campaign for us and the income we made from it was about £35k, which provided a cash buffer of over six months. We were off and we hadn't needed to look for external investment.

At this point I realized we were more personally secure than we had ever been before. Even though our start-up business could still easily fail, we had enough money to pay ourselves for at least six months. In a job, you would be lucky to get three months' notice. So, our unstable start-up was actually more stable than we'd realized.

Call it a buffer or a war chest, all businesses need at least six months' money. It is amazing how you make better decisions when you feel confident you can sustain yourself.

Having a war chest of 6 months is always a good idea. It could be the difference between failure or survival.

Lesson 24: Hustling for growth. Why you should ask for business... but you can't hustle for ever

So what did we actually *do* to get Media21 off the ground? The best word I can find to describe our growth strategy is that we **hustled**. We called everyone we knew in the industry. We had a clear pitch – we could do it better than the big network agencies – even if our business was not really that different. Our clients got access to the kind of senior experience they would not otherwise get and that was a big draw for many. If I was really honest, we were still a consultancy at this stage. The agency part only came later once we had a team.

The other thing we did was to ask everyone for business: we didn't assume they knew we were hunting for it. The number of times people said "OK, we'll keep that in mind" was quite surprising. And people really did come back to us with new client leads.

Don't be afraid to ask contacts for business leads. I would regularly ask for an introduction to someone interesting I didn't already know. This networking helped us find new customers.

But, as Lesson 18 shows, hustling can only take you so far.

By hustling, we somehow managed to get on Dixons' radar. Their head of advertising agreed to see us, but I'm sad to say we wasted the opportunity. We simply did not prepare. Our view that the big agencies were doing it wrong did not make a convincing argument as to why Dixons should work with us – even if we were right. We talked too much about the market and ourselves and not once did we talk about how we could make a difference to Dixons' business. I see this regularly, companies talking about themselves and what they do rather than talking about how they can benefit the client.

We should have been smarter when trying to win customers. If we had taken the time to go over the Dixons business, pulling out a number of things they undoubtedly could have been doing better, and we had made suggestions how things could be improved, I think we could have generated some work. As it was, we were passionate but irrelevant.

Lesson 25: Don't be afraid to pivot. Especially if it is better for your customers

One day in 2011, Rhys said we needed to find an Agenda21 way of doing paid search. We were too reliant on third parties and it was not scalable. We had already started to bring our own service in-house and the arrival of our first large search customer gave us a large account to work with. This resulted in a left-field approach where we started to use and develop in-house a technology called SearchRev. If other search management technologies were like a small hatchback, SearchRev was like a Ferrari. It was hugely complicated but once we got to grips with it, it made a huge difference to campaign performance. And it meant that we were masters of our own destiny, less reliant on third party suppliers and able to tailor better what we offered our clients.

In essence, Google channels advertisers' money into the searches that make Google most money while still hitting campaign targets. SearchRev allowed us to bypass that and to buy the searches that we wanted to buy – hitting targets for the minimum cost. Google hated it. We took delight in the fact that Google didn't like our campaigns because they could not understand what we were doing. We loved it and so did our search customers. Even in a competitive search market like recruitment, our way of working gave them a double-digit percentage advantage.

Our work with SearchRev, and later with a newer piece of kit called Marin, meant that, without realizing it, we had stumbled upon an independent way of operating and our long-term approach. What appealed to clients, and what worked really well, was that the three of us were at the top of our game, free to be entrepreneurial and pivot – find that Plan B – when we needed to, relishing the opportunity to make a difference. We were hugely commercial in our dealings with clients and they loved it because we so often had a big impact on their business performance.

Lesson 26: It's not all glory scaling a business. Be prepared to roll up your sleeves

Starting a company means there are a lot of menial jobs to do. If you only want the status and the CEO job title, then be prepared for a shock. It may not be for you and, if you go into business with a partner like this, you are introducing another failure risk into the business.

As Agenda21 hired more people, my reality was another trip to Ikea to buy more desks, chairs and pot plants; an early morning visit on a Saturday to drop them off in Covent Garden, avoiding the traffic wardens and lugging everything up three flights of stairs. Even as an award-winning agency, we were still small and these things were not going to do themselves.

The arrival of new staff and a growing team meant the emergence of structure in our business – another part of us growing up. The three partners – Pete, Rhys and myself – multitasked in many areas and, at the time, that interchangeability was an asset. Later on, this lack of role definition would cause problems but, for now, we were growing well, adding more structure when we needed to – and rolling our sleeves up when something needed to be done.

Not that long ago, three very senior ad agency executives decided to start their own company. Reality bit quite quickly when the implications of having no PA, no drivers and a healthy dose of starting things from scratch hit home; going it alone was far harder than they ever anticipated. The phone really did not ring and they were all back in senior jobs inside six months. The point is that perception and reality can differ significantly. Saying you are an entrepreneur is easy. Assembling furniture at 11pm on a Friday night is less so. Eyes open please.

Lesson 27: How to build successful joint ventures

In my experience, joint ventures (JVs) can be difficult. The theory is simple but things often derail in the execution. Over the years, we have worked with many partners, some formally and some informally. Many just wanted to take and others genuinely wanted to work together. What made our most successful JV with another agency work was true mutuality: we were both tied together and the JV fulfilled a requirement for both parties. Most importantly, neither party had the upper hand.

In spring 2007, the CEO of a big agency called Rapp approached us. They did not have much digital capability and wanted to buy us. We said there was not much to buy as we were still too young. What we really meant was we weren't finished yet and we only wanted to sell later and for more money when we were bigger. Rapp then floated an idea of a JV where we would provide digital services to them and their clients. In previous years they had spent a lot of money trying to build a digital team and had failed. Working with us meant they could access a credible team overnight. We could simply plug in.

So began our most formal and effective venture, built on the principle of mutually assured pain. Let me explain. We started working with them in a small way: we would share the costs and share the spoils. There was no contract and we treated Rapp like a client. They treated us as a white label to begin with – something we weren't happy about – but there were also benefits. Eventually, we became a more integrated part of the company and had people working in each other's offices. It worked incredibly well. We helped Rapp win business with digital credibility; we got to work on clients that ordinarily would not have considered a small independent. Very quickly it became apparent to both parties that the arrangement worked and there would also be considerable pain (financial for Agenda21 and skills for Rapp) for both parties should the arrangement end. It was brilliantly simple and it worked.

Lesson 28: Growth phase: building a money-making machine

When Agenda21 really got going, I realized we were getting near to being a money-making machine. It was not an aim of ours to begin with. We were motivated more by being masters of our own destiny; none of the three of us aspired to the kind of job where you could never be off duty. But changing our perspective was a crucial step in moving away from being just a consultancy business, ever reliant on the founders to operate.

Instead of Pete, Rhys and me doing everything, we started to build a quality team around us, introducing a company structure around our business management functions, mainly by building client teams. As we built on our reputation and won more new clients by networking like crazy and winning awards, gradually the business became less reliant on the three founders.

The point here is this. To begin with the three of us were doing all of the work that needed to be done but, with only so many hours in the day, we would ultimately be limited in how much work we could do and therefore how much money we could make. We didn't really have a business yet; we were, in reality, three very busy freelance consultants.

The first stage in building the machine was to hire someone who could help us to be more productive. That meant someone to do the day-to-day work so that we could focus on finding customers and making money. It felt like the biggest leap going from three freelancers to becoming an employer; most companies I've worked with leave this decision far too late. I can understand why it happens; confidence in the future is a big factor, but, sometimes, you just have to take the leap.

By freeing ourselves up we also could focus on generating the extra cash we needed to fund new employees. It's not quite investing in machinery (and of course, we didn't treat people like machines), but the principle is the same. Our second hire was less focused on day-to-day tasks and, increasingly, we built a team who could operate with increasing autonomy – again, freeing us up to win new customers.

And then, of course, our autonomous teams meant we could build a service machine without us founders having to be involved. The teams were obviously directed by us, but, before long, they needed only minimal input. We set the parameters within which they could work.

This model is scalable up to a good size where you can then improve productivity using technology. It meant we could begin to make money while we slept because our team could deliver the work within the structure that we had built. Once we got to this stage, I was struck – while having a beer in the pub opposite the office – that the work was still going on without me. The machine was up and running.

SCALE

Chapter 3

Lessons for scale: the coming-of-age phase

This section is about building proper organization and structure that will set you up for growth, both in size and in values. Your own values and those of your company may be similar but this is the point where your company takes on its own personality. Being less dependent on the founders is a good thing as you are creating a robust company that is built to last.

At this stage, the company is more like a machine you've built, able to operate autonomously. But you still need to find the right data levers to control it. It is important to stay focused as it is easy to get distracted. You may even receive opportunistic approaches to sell.

If the machine is running well you may even have time and money to entertain opportunities you previously didn't have time for. It can be a mixed blessing so take care.

Lesson 29: Perception is reality #1: how an office move can re-invigorate growth

Agenda21's first office was in Long Acre in Covent Garden and it felt like a house – because technically it was. Despite moving into other floors of the building we rapidly outgrew the space and, after a few years, we moved to offices in the Heal's Building on Tottenham Court Road. I was amazed at how, the minute we arrived, Agenda21 felt like a different company. We had a space that felt the way a media agency should feel: a bright, open-plan loft space in Central London which was buzzing with people. Light and airy, it felt like we had legitimately arrived. It is funny to think that, up to then, we had done great work, we had a great team and had won awards, but it was moving into a nice office that made us feel like a real company. It's true what they say: perception is reality and I sometimes wonder whether an earlier move would have accelerated our growth more quickly.

More recently, at Goodstuff, we trialled a day where people drew lots to decide where they would sit that day. It meant people mixed up and moved around, spoke to different people and I am convinced that new ideas were born. It was so popular that it's now a monthly event.

People and companies can get easily get stale and this can be a drag on growth. It can be difficult to keep the energy of a small company as you grow but something as simple as a desk move or a tidy up can have a profound effect on a business and its culture.

Lesson 30: Perception is reality #2: your brand is far more important than you realize

It really ought to be down to the quality of work companies do, but, often, it isn't. We may not all be marketers, but we all have customers and they have expectations.

At the Goodstuff agency, one of the founders told me just how much time and money they put into making their offices look amazing; it's a big part of how they position themselves. I think my businesses would have benefitted from marketing themselves better and earlier; it is my biggest single regret that we did not build a marketing team – and a brand – earlier. Ultimately, when your company is valued for investment or sale, having strong marketing and positioning can have a big impact on any multiple of valuation: much of the desirability of a company can be associated with its brand appeal to customers.

Agenda21 could definitely have done better with its marketing. It was never a strong point, as the three of us did not like blowing our own trumpets; instead, we preferred to let the quality of our work do the talking. That meant awards were important to us and we had good visibility within the industry, but we weren't really that visible (or differentiated) with customers. Just being a digital agency was no longer enough. We lacked a clarity of purpose: our clear vision for digital (and how it should be done) did not translate into a customer proposition that was relevant and appealing to clients. We had been flattered by our growth and award wins made us feel invincible. It was a mistake – not terminal – but one that felt like a number of opportunities missed.

We learned that great marketing and a strong brand can make it easier to grow by appealing to potential customers, even in a B2B market. I'm amazed at how much inbound business comes into Goodstuff simply because they are clearly positioned in their market. Don't make my mistake: invest early in your brand and in sales and marketing. Relying on the efforts of the founders is not always enough.

Lesson 31: Do you really need a non-executive? Or should you be looking elsewhere?

As we were growing Agenda21, we kept thinking that something was missing. We were working well together and there was a huge amount of respect between us, but we didn't yet have a machine that could function without us – and that was what we would need to build for the business to scale further.

We had been introduced to a potential non-executive director who had previously built and sold his own agency and we liked him a lot. We decided to bring him on board. While he was generous and diligent with us, his appointment changed the dynamic of our board and not for the better.

I ended up hating board meetings at this time and deliberately missed two. Our non-exec's presence meant that we did not have the full and frank discussions we used to have. Up to then our board meetings were slightly disorganized, but they were always co-operative and we made decisions. It became clear that having a non-exec director at that time was not right for us and we made the decision to part company with him. In fact, to his credit he had also realized this and said he would "fall on his sword". In fact, far from doing anything wrong, he had shown us we were a strong team capable of making decisions.

We realized at that point that what we were really missing was a proper sales and marketing function.

It is often easy to grow dissatisfied with what you have and there is always the attraction of things new and shiny. We were looking for something, but we ended up looking in the wrong place. What we thought we were missing was in fact nothing of the sort. We were a strong management team and pretty rounded. What we really needed was to win more new clients, and the simplest solution was, as so often, the right one. We just needed to grow sales.

Lesson 32: Everyone needs an elevator pitch. Here's how to write one

I once attended a training session where the guest speaker spoke about perfecting your elevator pitch. Over the day we worked on how we could present a compelling pitch in just 30 seconds. It was one of my most memorable sessions.

I started the day thinking we already had a good proposition but realized when I presented my pitch to such a brutally honest audience that I was wrong. My first effort was a mess. That said, so was everyone else's. Over the session we all honed our pitches and focused in on the really unique and compelling message around what we could offer. When I presented at the end of the day, I nailed it and it felt amazing. For the first time, I felt able to talk about Agenda21 in a clear and compelling way.

The perfect elevator pitch is in three parts and should be no more than 60 seconds in length.

> Your opening: What can you say in the first 10 seconds to grab a customer's attention?
>
> Show not tell. Give an example or story to illustrate the benefits of what you're offering.
>
> Your ending: What's the memorable line you want to leave them with?

Ours read like this:

> *We use our forensic analysis process to deliver what we call the Agenda21 guarantee. We guarantee to improve your performance by at least 15% or we'll refund our fees.*

For example, for company X we took some of their TV budget and ran it online. For no extra spend we delivered an extra £360,000 worth of sales (emphasis on the £360,000).

So, for you, Mr Client, we have identified that area XYZ could be improved. Let's talk about your business.

We set to work and attended a client agency speed dating afternoon hosted at Chelsea Football Club. Previously I'd been cynical about these events and, in typical hustling fashion, we would have attended an event like this with minimal preparation. Confident in our digital credentials, we would turn up and talk. Not this time. This time I insisted we prepared properly. Pete wasn't happy as he really did like to turn up and simply talk. But that was the whole point for me. At a certain size, clients don't just want to buy into one individual. They want to buy into a team.

I did the preparation work as I was confident this approach was right. I knew the others would never do any prep work, but I also knew they would buy into it once they saw it in action. I insisted we used the elevator pitch and, for each client we were to see, we had a clear point of view around what the last sentence should cover. In other words, we reviewed their business as best we could and identified where we could make a difference. And we nailed it. The feedback we got from the day was that we were the most impressive agency there.

It all sounds so obvious now but at the time it wasn't.

I learned that having a clear sales and marketing message is crucial. We should also have invested in a dedicated sales and marketing function earlier. Other, more sales-focused companies grew faster than us, even though we were better. Having a dedicated resource, whose sole function was to get our story out there, was a huge step forward for us. Leaving it so late in our development was one of our key mistakes.

Lesson 33: Insight can be an effective way to engage with potential customers

These days, in most industry sectors, ramping up sales is not just a matter of making X number of cold calls per day; on its own, that simply won't work anymore. Your ideal customer is also somebody else's ideal customer and people can be bombarded with sales messages. So how to cut through?

Just as you don't go from meeting someone to getting married straight away, in business there often needs to be a period of getting to know one another before a customer will buy your product or sign on the dotted line for your services. That's why a regular exchange of high-quality insight – something that potential customers will value – supports early engagement and interaction that can pave the way. Make sure you do offer something relevant and useful like research projects, white papers or regular market updates. All can offer value to customers who are keen to gain an advantage – and they can make you stand out. The value exchange is key.

Regularity means familiarity and an opportunity to build a conversation. Larger companies often use white papers to generate email leads but a more personal approach can work well for start-ups and growing companies. A friend of mine put this to great use when he was starting his own company. He spent quite a lot of money on a credible research company to conduct research and he then used the research to open doors to potential customers who would not otherwise have spoken to such a small company. It's a great example of a marketing-led approach to sales rather than sales by numbers.

Lesson 34: Get the right management information and use it to inform your decision making

I have always been really hot on getting invoices out of the door (I often think it is the best part of the job as it means we are getting paid) and paying our suppliers (simply the right thing to do). But, as we grew, we lacked decent financial reporting – we were penny pinching and managing the detail, but we really didn't know where we were financially. We really struggled to get any kind of management reporting so we could understand how the business as a whole was faring.

I remember at one point saying we were running the business based on our forecast. What that meant was that, even though we knew what our income from clients was and had a sense of our major costs, we really didn't know where we were in aggregate. But I learned that we needed more rigorous management information that we could use to make good decisions. We just weren't making as much money as we should have been. As is so often the case, we went a bit crazy on the hiring front. It was nothing terminal, but it was enough to give us a shock and make us think again about getting the right information in place so that we could see the bigger picture.

I still see companies running without that same kind of financial rigour. In service-based businesses like ours it means two things: you can easily end up hiring too many people and it's easy to end up with too many people in the wrong places and not enough people where you really need them.

This was another lesson in growing up. We were moving away from being a simple single-revenue/profit centre where we could judge the business as a whole and "wing it". We needed to get serious about using the right management information to manage the business better. Like the dials on an aircraft, I imagined a dashboard that would enable me to measure the right information to see how the business was progressing. My levers were:

Pipeline (number and size of potential customers) – how much we could grow in all likelihood

Pitch-to-win ratio – how good we were at converting new prospects into customers

Billings (turnover) per head – a measure of how productive we were

Income-to-salary ratio – a measure of how profitable and productive we were

Extraction rate (gross margin) – how good we were at charging customers

Net margin – how profitable we were.

Our monthly reporting showed these figures and, more importantly, by looking at them on a rolling 12- month basis, we could see trends and react accordingly. So, for example, if our pipeline started to dip, we could see it happening and try to deal with it.

Many sales-based companies use tools like Salesforce to build these kinds of reports, but, as these tools are almost infinitely customizable, reporting can all too easily become too complicated. One company I worked for had allowed this to happen. With too many people contributing – all with their own requirements – I inherited a Salesforce deployment that had become a monster. And it was not really telling us what we needed to know. Simplicity and clarity are key here: work out what you really need to know in order to understand and build your business and build your reporting accordingly. For many companies, this kind of thing can happily run in a spreadsheet. Don't let tools like Salesforce lead you into ever-growing complexity; keep things as simple as you can.

Lesson 35: How building a coaching culture can help you avoid problems before they become critical

Shouty command and control has never been my leadership style. It might work for some but I have always thought you get the best out of people by supporting them. I always try to hire for attitude and train for skills. A culture based on fear means that people are more likely to hide problems and, with inexperienced people, there is the added issue of just not seeing ahead.

At Agenda21, I instigated a coaching programme with all the team heads, eight people in all. I undertook to spend an hour per week with each person, on a one-to-one basis. For 20 minutes, we would cover current work; a second 20 minutes would be about future work, and the last 20 minutes was for anything else they wanted to discuss. There are a range of coaching techniques that work, but I like and use CIGAR:

> C – Context. Talk to me about what the problem is.

> I – Ideal outcome. If you could wave a magic wand, what would happen?

> G – Gap. What is preventing this from happening?

> A – Action. What are you going to do in that case?

> R – Review. When do we relook at this?

It was quite a commitment for me, but it yielded far more than I expected. People opened up and often personal issues were raised too. I think people appreciated someone who would listen. More important was something I did not expect – it flushed out challenges when I asked one of my favourite questions: "What's keeping you awake at night?"

The response was frequently a background problem with the potential to flare up. Often, the person didn't really want to admit to it or didn't realize it was serious. From there we could work through a remedy and, *voila*, problem averted. It meant, for example, that the few years of Agenda21 leading up to the sale were far smoother than they might have been. Taking a coaching approach made a real difference to company outcomes as well as improving our culture.

Lesson 36: Challenge decisions to help you make better ones

I was fortunate enough to see David Marquet speak at a conference. David is the author of *Turn the Ship Around*, the story of how he unexpectedly took command of the submarine USS Santa Fe when its Captain quit, even though he and his crew had originally trained for a year to understand every aspect of how the submarine USS Olympia worked – a different class of submarine entirely.

A month into operations, during a simple drill, the Captain ordered "ahead two-thirds". The Officer on Deck repeated the order. Nothing happened. Marquet noticed that the Helmsman looked unsettled. When asked, the Helmsman pointed out there was no two-thirds ahead on this submarine. The Officer on Deck admitted he had repeated the order, even though he knew it was wrong.

Marquet realized that the usual leader–follower environment meant his crew would follow any order he gave, even though they knew it was wrong. In other circumstances this could be catastrophic. He decided to try a different kind of leadership: one based on intent. He gave subordinates his broad intentions, treated the crew like leaders and handed over to them control to make their own decisions to achieve his intent. It wasn't long before the USS Santa Fe went from the worst-performing submarine in the US Navy to the best and produced more submarine officers than any other.

What stuck with me was the idea that confirmation bias – company groupthink – can easily creep into an organization and lead to the kind of situation where everyone agrees on a decision (usually the CEO's) regardless of whether it is right or not. Poor decisions can be costly; take the example of Coca-Cola launching New Coke when everyone was perfectly happy with the original. Even the smartest companies can get caught out if nobody feels like they can challenge a poor decision.

My first run-in was at Media21 where, during the dot-com crash, we pinned our hopes for income on winning a client that we codenamed Project Clam (it was oil company Shell) when, in reality, it was nothing more than a lead – and a lukewarm one at that. Kidding ourselves that it was a possibility meant we could delay the unpleasant decision of laying people off. In the end, we convinced each other because it was what we wanted to believe.

More recently, I applied what we called a Red Team when tendering for a large contract. Alongside the team working on the tender, we also put another person onto the project who would not be involved in the day-to-day work but would instead regularly check in to challenge the thinking and approach of the tendering team. If the core team is convinced that a choice is the right one, then the Red Team will challenge them to make sure the choice really does stand up.

If you make it safe for people to challenge decisions, you are more likely to make better ones.

Lesson 37: Remove the temptation for fraud wherever you can

With a growing company, it's tempting to become hands off with your finance team but that can be a mistake. It is easy to focus elsewhere with a finance team that is running smoothly, but there are regular high-profile cases of internal fraud and it can cause disaster both financially and in terms of credibility and reputation.

Although I had no reason to suspect anyone, I was concerned that the opportunity was there for someone in finance to either authorize fraudulent payments or to pay fraudulent invoices. So, we put in place some basic checks and balances to make sure this couldn't happen. For example, we became (and remained) very hands-on with payments: two partners had to sign any cheque that was for more than £50 and Rhys took over checking and authorizing online payments.

We also put in place guidelines to give our management team more autonomy around spending. I've always been sceptical about giving people a budget because, funnily enough, the budget will always be spent – regardless of whether it is needed or not. That said, we categorized clients as small, medium and large in order to set expectations around things like entertaining clients based on the income we made. And we also put in place a company training budget set at a fixed 2% of our income, which enabled us to tie training to growth.

Fortunately, we never had a fraud problem. Whether that was down to our precautions or just good luck we will never know, but what I do know is that we didn't lose any money to fraud. Thinking about financial checks and balances is a good habit to develop early, and, once established, these protocols will continue to serve you well as you grow.

Lesson 38: The resource trap: how to ensure you have the right resources in the right places

Not all companies have the luxury of being awash with cash to invest for scale. Most of my companies have had very little investor cash and we have grown using our own cashflow. It meant we did not grow as quickly as we could, but it did mean that we owned more of the company as a result. Given the choice between owning 100% of a self-funded business or a tiny amount of a funded business, I would always choose the former.

As Agenda21 approached its fifth year, we were falling into a classic resource trap; it was becoming harder to know when and where to bring in more people. Getting it wrong meant we would have too many people in the wrong places – and would cost us profit. Not enough people where you need them had the potential to hold back growth. Like any production line, you want to get the most out of your assets (in this case people, but equally machines) before you bring in extra capacity.

Worse, in a people business, you can be swayed by those people and teams who shout loudest about needing more people. Rather than the business having an empirical measure, I was at risk of making bad decisions based on influence and emotion.

I went back to basics and applied my **Golden Rule of Making Money in Business**:

One pound of salary attracts one pound of overhead.

This means that your salary bill cannot be more than half of your income. It really is that simple. Any more than that and you are losing money. A properly productive team should be able to process enough work in a week, month or year to cover twice their costs (ie salary and overhead). Ideally, you'd add in a margin for profit but the 50/50 rule of thumb is a useful basic ready reckoner.

So, for example, if I win a new customer that will generate an extra £100k of income it doesn't mean we can hire people to the value of £100k. It means our salary bill can be no more than £50k. The remainder then covers all the other overheads in the business. In our case, the reality was our overheads were nowhere near this percentage, so we had a natural profit margin built in too.

I've used this in all my businesses and it's the single reason we have made money. I was able to understand the relationship between the work we do, how much to charge clients and how much resource we could allocate.

In fact, I have used it again at Goodstuff where my number 2, using this technique, made a great commercial call. He had two extra people planned for an annual budget but, when it came to it, he decided not to hire one of them because the Golden Rule showed he didn't need them. Most people in that situation and without the rule would want as much resource as possible – regardless of the cost – and that's where company profits often end up.

It is so important that you understand your business. Otherwise other people (who have different agendas) will end up deciding for you.

The Golden Rule applies on the downside too. If your income is falling then your costs need to follow suit too. That said, government support to furlough people means that redundancies are not inevitable. Resource, and more importantly skills and goodwill, will be retained in businesses to deal with the recovery.

Well-run and well-differentiated companies will be far better placed to weather the storm so make sure yours is one of them. I don't know what kind of country and economy we will be on the other side but I do know that getting the basics right will keep you in as strong a position as possible.

And don't forget that companies as diverse as Salesforce, Microsoft, Uber and AirBnB all launched during downturns. Societies change during a downturn and new opportunities can arise so now might be a good time to start something too

Lesson 39: Diversification: take care when launching or investing in other businesses

As Agenda21 grew up in the early 2010s, we started to feel very clever as business owners and success felt very natural. We had won awards, we had a team of around 35 people and we were profitable. Around the same time, we co-launched a new business: a mobile advertising company. We backed the individual concerned and offered support with office space, back office functions and hopefully access to new business – much as Deepend did with us a decade earlier.

The mobile company was aiming to capitalize on the growth in mobile use (the first iPhone had only launched two or three years earlier) and the plan was to advise large companies on how to operate in this new area. We looked at a 60/40 deal, with the founder having the greater share. On paper it was a great idea, but expectations on both sides were different. They were expecting significant input from us, but we were busy with our day jobs at Agenda21. We were expecting just to "house" them and offer back office services. With hindsight, we probably took too much and gave back too little. The founder was frustrated and said that if we were not going to contribute then there was no point us being shareholders. Sadly, we had to agree and we signed our shares back.

We had committed the cardinal sin of failing to set clear expectations around our relationship, especially when it came to things like exactly how much of my time they were expecting and what I was able/prepared to do. Getting a great headline deal that doesn't survive is ultimately a bad deal, no matter how swashbuckling you might feel.

We had a similar experience when investing in a new tech venture of an old acquaintance. This felt like a very grown-up thing to do but, even though the company went well, subsequent rounds of funding meant that, short of investing more out of our own pockets, our share of the business would be diluted more and more. In the end, the company was acquired and we were left with illiquid shares in a company we'd never heard of.

Rhys hit the nail on the head when he said the only successful investments we ever made were those in ourselves. Looking back, every other venture outside Agenda21's core business required either more time or money than we were able to give. We were in danger of allowing ourselves to be spread too thinly. Putting ourselves in a situation where our time was needed elsewhere just didn't make sense. It's a scalability problem common in service businesses. Clients buy into you, the founder or team. But there is only so much to go around and getting distracted is dangerous. We learned that what worked for us was to stick to our knitting. Better to do one thing well than many things badly.

Lesson 40: Pick your battles: when to let a legal challenge go

Our DataShaka business was originally called Media Science. One day we got a letter from a legal firm representing a company in Dallas saying we were in breach of trademark for using the name Media Science, which belonged to them. It was a typically aggressive legal challenge: they wanted us to stop using the name within two months and we needed to respond within two weeks or they would start to take legal action against us.

I don't like being pushed around and when I checked them out and saw that they were a market research company who conducted focus group research for their customers, I was annoyed. Their business was nothing to do with the kind of data-led processing work we were doing with Media Science. They seemed to operate in a completely different trademark category.

But, while I was strongly motivated to fight it, the idea of arguing with a potentially litigious US company and getting caught up in an expensive and lengthy legal argument was not appealing. We had recently put principle first by defending a legal claim – on the basis that we felt we were in the right – rather than settling earlier. It cost us much more in time and energy than we recouped financially.

In this case, we all agreed that the best course of action was to change name, and we took the opportunity to find a different name that better reflected what the company did. The company wasn't just media and it wasn't really science – more data and technology. We ran through around 50 different names before we settled on one that reflected what the company did, was not being used already and was available to buy cheaply. DataShaka (pronounced shaker) was born.

After facing two legal battles, we learned to pick our battles wisely. Don't underestimate the distracting effect of these kinds of arguments. I hate it, but I have learned that these kinds of challenges are a fact of life in business. Unless settling will cause harm to your company, then avoiding a legal fight is often the better way to go. Legal challenges can drag on; let them go and keep focused on growing your business. And don't be afraid to turn a problem into an opportunity to create something better.

Lesson 41: The potential downside of a successful JV

Lesson 27 tells the story of the one joint venture that really worked for us, with the agency Rapp. We worked together on a pretty informal basis for six years: quite simply, we shared costs and spoils using a joint P&L. There were Rapp people and Agenda21 people working for the JV and we accounted for their costs and overheads on the P&L. Once both sides had their costs accounted for the remaining profit was split equally. Overall the relationship worked well. In fact, it was almost like the second round of funding we never needed to secure. At one point we were earning something like £30k a month in income from the JV, giving us a capital cushion we could use to grow.

It was a great problem to have. We managed the potential for distraction by putting only Rhys into the JV so that we didn't have too much founders' time swallowed up. A bigger risk for us was that, if Rapp became too big a proportion of our income, we would become overly reliant on them. It would also be unlikely that any other company would ever buy us, as the Rapp business would disappear overnight. We were also concerned that the Rapp client income would never count towards the company valuation. If Rapp bought us, they would say they were not prepared to pay us for business they had given us – in other words they would discount the value of Agenda21 as they had helped us. Any other buyer would not be prepared to pay for business that would most likely stop on acquisition.

The takeaway here is that JVs can be useful, but also come with risks of distraction, a lack of enterprise value and of one party becoming overly dependent. Rapp provided us with really useful income and it enabled us to grow, but it could have gone the other way. We could have become addicted to Rapp and, unless we were able to grow the rest of the business as well (which we did), might have ended up being taken over by proxy.

Lesson 42: Building technology? Understand what you're getting into, and the skills you'll need

One of the constant challenges Agenda21 faced was around campaign reporting. The basic problem was that, when we ran a campaign, it took a huge amount of time to gather all the information about how the campaign had run and performed. For example, you can log in to Google and pull out a report. Then you log in to Facebook and pull another report. The two reports need to be combined and this usually involves manually taking the relevant bits and pasting them into a spreadsheet. As most campaigns would run in more places than just Google and Facebook, the work just got more complicated.

For me, it was crazy to have expensive people employed and sitting in the West End of London pulling reports and messing about with Excel. Most of my team would admit to spending all their time making a report and having no time left over to draw any insights from it.

After unsuccessful attempts at outsourcing, and with no proprietary software on the market, reporting was becoming a big productivity issue for us. So, we decided to build the system ourselves. We hired our first Chief Technology Officer, Phil Harvey, to help us build a platform to automate our reporting.

Phil's brief had two fundamental pillars. We needed to get data from different sources harmonized – not just able to show them on the same page – so that we could compare, say, Google with Facebook. And second, we didn't know what new sources of data would be available in the future, so the platform would need to be flexible enough to accommodate new sources quickly and easily. This set off a chain of events that led to a whole new spin-off tech company called DataShaka.

I had never run a tech team before and much of the first few weeks involved Phil and me getting to know each other and trying to get a grip on the task. Phil was at great pains to call himself a Systems Analyst (as opposed to a developer). What he meant was that, as well as developing product, he could also understand the broader context of what we were trying to do. He could anticipate where there was a conflict between what we were asking and what we really needed and he was a godsend. We started prototyping a dashboard we called D-View, which was really just a spreadsheet but populated with our two biggest campaign tools – Google and our adserver. It was looking good and we even showed it to joint venture partner, Rapp.

Working with Phil taught me that there is a world of difference between general management and project management. Many non-tech companies simply manage their work: it is iterative, people-based and focuses on assigning work and organizing people to a deadline. Project management is an entirely different discipline that requires a level of rigour and structure that most people simply don't appreciate. When dealing with large-scale projects, understanding the discipline needed for proper project management can really help to avoid or minimize cost and timing over-runs.

Phil also taught us the difference between product and engineering disciplines. Engineering will do what you tell them and then stop. Product people will interpret what you need and brief an engineering team to build it. For people without a tech background, like me, it's really important to be clear about what you need. Fortunately, we stumbled across Phil who could do both.

Lesson 43: Opportunistic approaches versus a planned exit. When should you start thinking (seriously) about an exit?

With Media21, we didn't have an exit plan in mind. In fact, it could not have been further from our minds, perhaps hardly surprising as we were only 18 months old when we had our first approach. With Agenda21 we learned the lesson and gave ourselves almost two years to get ready for an exit (see Lesson 57).

We were quite idealistic in our approach to Media21 – wanting to do good work, wanting to work with like-minded clients, wanting to push the boundaries and do new things. It laid bare the idea that, if there was a buyer out there, they would have to be the right buyer. Our attitude meant that people were generally supportive. That's what got us so many recommendations. But, as the word spread, this also generated interest from potential buyers. In late 1999, we were approached by two US companies – both wanted us to be their bridgehead into Europe.

Over the next few months we had repeated meetings and conversations with these potential buyers. There wasn't a point where we decided it was right to sell – remember, we had been approached, not the other way around. The three of us were interested and keen to keep on talking but hadn't made the mental leap that a sale was desirable. It meant that the sale process and its aftermath felt more chaotic and rushed than it might have been – although we had no other point of reference at the time.

Looking back, I can see that Media21 got caught up in the hysteria of the dot-com boom. Most of us never encounter a market like that. If you do, then expect to have conversations based around future growth potential where the way your company is valued will be based more on views of the future than anything based on reality. Because of these exceptional market conditions, our lack of planning was not exposed and we were able to secure a lucrative deal. In more mature markets, exit planning is crucial, as it was when we sold Agenda21 (see Lesson 70).

Media21 was caught up in a gold rush and there was a huge dose of luck in the ultimate outcome. Agenda21 was a planned sale where we had time to build a company and remove many of the risks that could sour a deal, making sure we got good value and were more likely to be successful post-sale. Media21 was a company that was bought; Agenda21 was a company that was sold. In an ideal world you'd get both – a planned exit in an exuberant market – to maximize value.

Chapter 4

Lessons for scale: surviving tough times

Most people running a company will experience a slow-down or recession at some point. All slowdowns are different. For example, the dot-com bubble bursting in 2000 directly hit my industry and was felt severely. The credit crunch of 2008 did not play out the same way and in many ways was not as bad as I feared. Economic disruption will often throw up opportunities. However, whatever the reason, severity or impact of tough times, you need to survive in order to thrive.

When the dot-com bubble burst, it decimated my first company. Hopefully you won't experience anything as severe as that, but it is inevitable that all companies will experience tough times at some point. Whether it is the loss of a large customer to economic recession or the unintended consequences of government legislation, headwinds will come in many forms.

It's important to remember that strong, well-run businesses can and will survive – and even thrive – during a slowdown, even though it can feel very scary at the time. It was Warren Buffet who said that a rising tide flatters everyone: it's only when the tide falls that you can see who is not wearing any clothes. In short: solid businesses are more able to survive a slowdown. Ensure you're well run and make your decisions based on what you can actually see rather than the fear often portrayed in the media. Equally, do not be surprised to see companies with too much debt or those who do not serve their market well struggle and fail.

So, what does a well-run business look like and how can you thrive during a downturn?

Lesson 44: Showtime

Your team will pay a disproportionate amount of attention to your behaviour at work – even if you don't realize it – and this can impact morale. When things get tough, it's easy to allow your worries to broadcast to the rest of the company, especially if you work in an open-plan office.

It is important to remember that your role as leader is to be the front person in your company; your worries cannot be allowed to impact negatively on team morale.

I call it **Showtime**. At Agenda21, I would stop on the stairs on my way into the office, pause and say to myself "It's show-time" and breeze into the office with a smile and a "Good morning, everyone" – even if I felt terrible. It's code for: people look to you for guidance, and if you're unhappy they will be unhappy; if you're anxious they will be anxious too.

Never let your own stress or anxiety show to your team. They will have their own worries and will often think things are worse than they really are if they see you behaving negatively.

I've been involved with two companies where the leader has struggled to keep a lid on things. I once saw the horror on people's faces when a leader bashed his keyboard with his fists in frustration when going through a rough patch. Worse was a leader who, again during a rough patch, took out his frustra-tions on his management team by singling out an individual on what seemed to be a two-weekly cycle. Behind his back everyone was discussing who would be getting it next. Bad for motivation and bad for staff retention.

Lesson 45: Be brutally realistic about how much business is on the horizon

After we sold Media21, one thing was becoming very clear: there were no clients coming to us from our US parent company. We were very much on our own.

Our head count had risen to about 40 people and we had assimilated a team from the US, mostly on the expectation of new business. Most of our clients were dot-com companies for whom success at that point meant arrivals, views and website visits. Results were strong, company targets were being hit. Investors kept on investing and budgets kept on flowing.

What we weren't seeing, however, was the prospect of new clients. Until that time, growth had just happened naturally and we had not had to worry too much about where new clients would come from. But now the pipeline was running dry.

With our new owners and the promise of new clients, we had ended up making decisions we would not otherwise have made. Now we had too many people and not enough business.

The tricky thing to figure out at the time was whether we were experiencing a blip or a trend. Our innate optimism made it difficult for us to believe that things would not continue as they had up to that point – we were successful businessmen after all. Being in the market also made it harder to see the bigger picture, something like not seeing the wood for the trees. We simply hoped new business would pick up. But what we hoped was just a blip turned out to be a trend. Naïve optimism meant we didn't plan for the worst-case scenario. The combination was not positive.

This is probably the biggest lesson I've ever learned and it has become a constant for me: I only forecast income from known clients and for known amounts. New business isn't factored into my forecasting. If there's doubt about a client or a budget then I'll use the lower amount. Forecasting costs is easy; they are more predictable. Forecasting income is trickier and the risk of overstatement means you can easily be left with too many people who are expensive to hire, expensive to fire and can cause mischief if underemployed. Far better to staff up when new income arrives.

We were running at a loss. All the reforecasting in the world could not change the reality that we didn't have the income to cover our costs. We were forecasting for new business that was not going to materialize. And as the dot-com market started to unravel, extraordinary things started to happen. One client simply disappeared over a weekend – a viable customer one day and gone the next. Income was falling off a cliff.

By constantly reforecasting potential new business, we were hoping to buy time until new business came in or hoping for our US parent to magic something up. If we had been more honest with ourselves, we would have acknowledged that neither was going to happen any time soon.

Lesson 46: Bite the bullet – sometimes redundancies are better than endless uncertainty

Running at a loss is not a sustainable place to be in business. When the dot-com bubble burst, we had no option but to lose some Media21 staff. In a small company, it was clear something was up. It was impossible to hide and, in an open-plan office, it was tricky to talk openly to make the necessary plans. At the time, if you were making more than 15 people redundant, employers needed to give a two-week consultation period. Even though we were below this number, we decided to run things by the book as it felt like the right thing to do. It was a big mistake.

When we sat everyone down to notify them of the job losses and consultation period, we thought we were doing the right thing. The consultation required that we would consult over a two-week period during which time we would agree with the staff who would go. We knew the people who were going and we knew the people we wanted to stay but, once committed to the process, we had to see it through and consult with everyone as to who should stay and who should go.

It destabilized the whole team. It was as if we had put everyone on notice; naturally every single person reconsidered their position. Every single person forgot about their day job and our business ground to a halt. News got out to the trade press, so we also had journalists sniffing around. Halfway through, one of the team came to us and said, "Please just tell us who's going and who's staying – it's killing us not knowing." He was the only one talking sense.

We did the best thing we could have done in the circumstances. We split people into two groups, the leavers and the stayers, and we notified everyone at the same time. Stayers were safe; they could get back to their work. Leavers were told they'd be paid their notice and would leave immediately.

Once the leavers had gone, we sat what was left of the team down and talked about how we were going to move forward.

Clients were reassigned and notified. Desks were cleared and we discussed the plan of getting closer to our parent company, MediaCom.

We got it right in the end but it took almost a week to get there. The damage was severe but it could have been worse. Our biggest fear was the company entering into a downward spiral of losing more people and losing clients, meaning we'd need to lose more people again.

We learned that even the closest-knit teams can easily be destabilized. We wanted to do the right thing by all of our team, but, for us, and with such a small group of people, the process of consultation was not working. It was better to let the leavers go quickly.

As a business leader the last thing you want to do is admit defeat and let people go. Employees often know far more about what's going on than you realize and often the best thing you can do is deal with the issue head on and focus on the people who are going to be staying.

Lesson 47: Never make a loss. It means you will never lose control

Once Media21 had started to lose money, our loss of control was sudden and events began to move quickly. Although we still had a fundamentally viable business – not all of our clients were dot-com companies – our poor grip on our finances came back to bite us. We didn't have at hand the information we needed to take back control – and, crucially, we were losing money.

Our decision to hire more people had changed the whole nature of the business. When the recession hit and income fell, we had nowhere to go. Our MediaCom conversations continued, and it was made clear that we could stay where we were (as an independent division) and go into liquidation or join our parent with a small team whose costs could be covered by our income. We had few options and it split us up as a leadership team; Rick decided against the move, but Pete and I went ahead. It felt like the end of an era, a rollercoaster that mirrored the fortunes of the dot-com companies we had hitched our business to. We still had our business, but we had lost control and there were only two of us left. Things would never be the same again.

More recently, I have seen this with a technology company with whom I work. The UK Division has started losing money and the investors are making noises about sidelining and possibly removing the CEO who has spent many years building up the business. It is very harsh, but would be almost impossible if the company was profitable; if the company was making money, it is likely the investors would be happy with the CEO's performance.

The irony from my point of view was that, six months after we had integrated Media21 into MediaCom, we were profitable again and making money. It is amazing how much more positive you feel from being in this position of strength. I have never lost a penny of profit since then.

Lesson 48: Use the Power of Three to maintain focus and direction

This revelation came initially from some presentation training with a television newsreader. She said that people only remember three things so, when it comes to building presentations, then you should focus on the three main things you want the audience to remember.

I took this idea further and gave everyone and everything three things to focus on. It came in very handy when I was working with an ad technology company. Things were so complicated there – way more than necessary – and the whole leadership team lacked clarity and focus. The company was not making money. In a classic sign of a team under pressure, they started lots of initiatives, constantly moving on to the next new thing while finishing nothing. It was made worse by the fact that the leadership team didn't have clarity around their roles and what was expected of them. Advising them properly would have taken weeks and I didn't want to hang around.

As a shortcut I sat down with the CEO and worked out the three most important things the business needed to focus on to build revenue. Then I worked with the leadership team to identify the three most important things in their respective areas that would contribute to the overall company goals.

My job then become one of policeman, ensuring everyone remained focused on their three objectives and nothing else. No distractions – a ruthless focus on the job in hand.

Did it work? In the year I worked with the company they made their first profit in years. It wasn't pretty, but it was effective. Sometimes, especially when times are tough, a ruthless focus on what really matters – in this case, it was driving revenue – needs to take priority over everything else.

Lesson 49: Every downturn is different. Sometimes you just need to sit it out

When the economy takes a turn, it's not always a surprise, but the downturn never works out in the way you expect. The post-2008 credit crunch was very different to the dot-com crash. And the next downturn will be different again.

I called the run-up to the credit crunch trading sideways because that was what it felt like. We were working as hard as ever in Agenda21, spinning lots of plates and yet financially the company didn't seem to be getting anywhere: our billings, income and profit all seemed to be static. And yet, we were winning more clients. I put it down to the impact of the financial crisis. My fear going into this recession was that, like the dot-com bust, we would lose clients overnight. Things did not develop in quite the same way. Rather than clients disappearing because they went bust or because they had their funding pulled, our more established clients simply cut back on spending without stopping it altogether, meaning the impact of the financial crisis was slower and more gradual than I feared.

Even though we were winning business, with each client spending less we were just plugging the gap in overall spend. Or income was flat year on year too. More clients, less spend, same amount of work. Agenda21 was better run than Media21 and that insulated us too. The 50% Golden Rule meant that, even though revenues were down, we were able to manage our resources better. We did OK, but it was frustrating. We felt we were not winning new clients of the calibre and size we thought we should. But, in the end, we just needed to be patient and sit it out until the economy recovered.

Lesson 50: The importance of investing in yourself. Why lifelong learning is important

In 2010 I went to a lunch held for company founders by the accounting firm Smith and Williamson. In passing, I asked the host where people like me should go for training, support and development. Without hesitation he said Vistage, a training and development programme for founders and CEOs. I got past the horribly corporate website, put a call in to them and subsequently met up with John Thorpe, who had been MD at General Electric – a real captain of industry. John chaired a group of around 15 people and I was invited to join. Looking back, it was the best thing I ever did.

The group met monthly. A typical day involved a morning session with a top-ranking guest speaker (including Simon Sinek and submarine commander David Marquet – see Lesson 36) talking about leadership from their own perspective, followed by afternoons given up to members' problems and issue solving. It wasn't cheap but I viewed it as the non-exec director we didn't need to hire. A number of key decisions and initiatives came directly from what I learned with Vistage. In fact, I would go further: it helped us to transform Agenda21 into a wonderfully profitable and saleable business.

One of my early initiatives was to introduce a coaching culture into Agenda21 (see Lesson 35). This was not about being nice to people. It was to help and support our senior team, many of whom were digital experts but inexperienced in building and developing their people. It was also a way for us to keep control of our senior team; through the coaching process we could anticipate problems they might not have spotted and deal with them before they became acute. Other initiatives like our PIP (Profit Improvement Programme; see Lesson 58) and honing our elevator pitch (Lesson 32) were critical in adding value into Agenda21.

Vistage provided me with ideas to improve the performance of Agenda21, so that, when the economic climate improved, we were ready to take advantage. I've never regretted the investment I made in Vistage and I've taken my own lifelong learning seriously ever since.

Lesson 51: Don't agonize over rates of staff turnover. Employees are more mobile than ever and people are going to leave

Businesses change and people do too. It's sometimes healthy for people to move on. We tried our hardest in this area and we seemed to employ three types of people: those who stayed longer, those who stayed shorter and those who were not right for us.

Although we had already moved from being a collection of doers into being a company with a structure and ethos, as a management team we were still behaving like a start-up where we micro-managed everything in the business. We three founders never saw this as a problem, but we learned that it was.

We brought in a head of talent and she proved to be a great asset. A key part of our development was the promotion of two senior colleagues to the Agenda21 board. It was one of our better moves. It meant that we had a mature layer of incredibly capable client management working alongside us. However, while it worked for us, it was incredibly frustrating for them, and one of them left us before much longer. We didn't give them enough autonomy in their day-to-day jobs, and they felt their contribution to our decision making was not important. Mature managers need the freedom to manage without day-to-day interference, something that was tough for our close-knit group of founders (see also Lesson 54).

We also had to manage high rates of staff turnover. One of the consequences of the credit crunch was the loss of opportunities for head-hunters in the financial sector. Many of them moved into the digital sector and started to aggressively target our staff. While this was the same for other agencies, it meant that we were paying hundreds of thousands of pounds each year in head-hunter fees to replace the people who were leaving us. I don't think we ever found a decent solution to this problem. Tightening up on our recruitment process to employ more suitable people didn't help and neither did additional training and career development options. The old adage of train your people so they can leave, but treat them so that they want to stay was something we totally bought into, but none of it helped. In the end we simply accepted it as part of us doing business and the head-hunter fees as a "tax" on our business.

Lesson 52: Stronger marketing will bring more sales and help you survive a downturn

I've mentioned before that my approach to new business tended to be haphazard at best. At Agenda21, we relied on our own networks to identify potential leads. Rhys and I used to spend a little bit of time trying to approach potential customers cold, but with little success. Most new clients came from recommendations. In the early days this was fine, and, to a certain degree, we had little choice. A resource-limited start-up has to hustle by making the most of what it has. But we weren't a resource-limited start-up anymore and, with the best will in the world, the three of us could not spend enough time on new business. In fact, for me, one of the signs of a business growing up is when the founders recognize the need for, and are able to surround themselves with, good people who bring new strengths and skills.

We hired our first head of marketing. He had a number of observations about our business, the main one being that we were better on the inside than we looked from the outside. It pointed to a lack of a consistent and co-ordinated marketing plan. And he was right: the three of us could hustle, but marketing always fell into the "important but not urgent" pile. Day-to-day work always got in the way.

He pulled us together around a theme of being slightly geeky, techy and scientific in the way we approached our work. It really did fit with who we were and how we operated. We started using the line *Agenda21 – Forensic Analysis* and we rallied around this message.

It felt that, for the first time, we had a clear position and a clear reason why clients should work with us. And it meant that, while we were surviving the downturn, we were getting clearer about why customers should choose us.

Lesson 53: How to identify and avoid poor-performing sales people

As we saw in Lesson 10, people tend to fall into two camps: hunters and farmers. Don't make the mistake of getting them mixed up. Never hire a farmer to do a hunting role. I've seen many companies get it wrong and, by the time you realize your mistake and put it right, it can have set your business back a year. I learned that it's a rule that has particular application for hiring sales and marketing people.

In one of my Vistage sessions, a new group member was talking about sales people. Chris ran an accounting software firm and had been part of a management buyout of the company. He talked about sales people being either hunters or farmers – sales people or marketing people – two sides of the same coin. Hunters hunt for new business. Farmers create the environment for sales leads to develop. If you're lucky you may be able to hire someone who can do both, but the reality is that most people will fall clearly into one camp or the other. Most companies need both functions but often make the mistake of trying to get a hunter to farm or, worse, a farmer to hunt.

With our messaging sorted out, we realized we needed a hunter too: someone to root out new business leads and help us grow.

Chris also had another brilliant tip – one of his hard-learned lessons. He asked potential sales candidates to show him their annual pay summary to see if their bonus payments really reflected their claimed performance. Sales people by their very nature are good at selling, so it can be difficult to separate the good ones from the bad ones. Your tax return doesn't lie.

Lesson 54: Hire slow and fire fast

It may seem obvious that it is better to take your time and hire carefully but, when the pressure is on, it's easy to cut corners. A classic mistake is hiring the person who is available right now as they don't have a notice period to work. I've seen a kind of group-think creep in where everyone convinces themselves it's the right candidate when what people are really saying is: we are really busy and we just want a person (any person) right now. If the person is not right for a job, they're not right. Expediency is never a sound recruitment strategy. Take the time you need to find the right person.

The opposite holds true when you need to let someone go. This is a hard step to take, and not one to be taken lightly, but this is also a case of needing to bite the bullet. Sometimes, a quick decision and a firm hand is what's needed. In one case, we employed someone who interviewed well and seemed to have a great "go-getter" attitude. However, he took the entrepreneurial thing too far in that he stopped doing the job he was supposed to do. He also seemed to be waging war with his boss. Both were new and it took me a while to unpick what was going on. I initially doubted the manager but it then became clear it was the employee who was causing problems. Rick and I took him into a meeting room on a Friday afternoon and we sacked him. My first time. Not a good feeling.

The point about firing fast is that the rest of the team will be well aware of how disruptive/lazy/problematic some people can be; even just one or two dissenters can disrupt a whole team. Failing to deal with a situation like this weakens your credibility and dilutes your authority. When we did eventually let this person go, the rest of the team asked: "What took you so long?" It is incredibly demotivating when people are working hard and see somebody else playing games. Move them on quickly.

Chapter 5

Lessons for scale: building scale for sale

If an exit is part of your company's plan then you will want to build a company with scale. Scale is good for two reasons. Obviously, a bigger company is more valuable than a smaller one. More importantly, a larger company will be more robust structurally, have a larger market footprint and hopefully momentum in sales growth – all things that remove risk for potential buyers. You can build scale specifically with a view to an exit but this can be dangerous if, for whatever reason, things don't go to plan. Sustainable growth is better – build the best company you can.

And if I have learned one thing about building scale it is this: the most important thing is getting the right people around you for this next stage of growth and then getting everyone facing the same direction and working towards the same goal.

It is going to be so much harder if you do not cede control of many aspects of the business to a wider range of people. It's not just about trust. You have to be ready and able to give up some control. Getting this wrong (as we did) can hamper growth. Succession plans and board member plans may also start to crop up: how do you build the next generation of leaders in the company?

Lesson 55: Your role as CEO

At the point where you are scaling up, it is easy to forget that, on top of the hundreds of day-to-day tasks, you also have a role that is scaling up too: that of being an MD or CEO. This entails three key roles:

1. Your job is to set the strategy for the company: the who, what, where, how of what you do and how you will make money.
2. You need to get the right people and resources on board to deliver the strategy.
3. You must communicate and champion the strategy to anyone and everyone inside and outside the business so that everyone is clear how they can contribute to the company's vision.

Why is this important? Aside from the obvious – that if you don't do it, nobody else will – it is vital that you are clear about where the company is going and how you are going to get there so that your team knows what it's aiming for.

It's easy to get bogged down in the day to day, especially when you're still growing, or when times are tough, but the most important thing you can do is lift your head and make sure you keep your eyes on that horizon. Others can support operations; you need to lead on strategy.

Lesson 56: The importance of scale: getting to £1m profit

M&A advisory company Results International had always said that Agenda21 would become a serious acquisition target once we were making £1m profit. That may be a psychological barrier, but it's also a sign of how grown-up a company has become.

There is no way a company can reach that level of profitability without having the right infrastructure in place around people, systems and sales. It's also a test of the management team.

There are lots of businesses that make a few hundred thousand pounds of profit. Getting above, say, half a million takes a business with a decent leadership and a good position in the market that is appealing to customers. Getting above a million is for businesses who have thought of everything. You can't wing it to a million; product, people, leadership, positioning and systems all need to be fully built and running like a well-oiled machine. Compared to the business we were when we started, when the founders *were* the business, we were now in a place where any of us could disappear and nothing bad would happen straight away. The business would continue and would continue to operate quite happily.

Understanding the £1m profit goal was a big lesson for us in the importance of scaling up.

Lesson 57: Why founder–shareholder alignment is critical

In the end, the decision to sell Agenda21 came at a fractious board meeting. We all agreed that being part of something bigger made a lot of sense as it would diversify our product offering to customers. Digital marketing was fragmenting and, while we were good at what we did, clients were increasingly looking for a wider range of services. We decided that we would start to get shipshape for sale.

Before that, however, we had disagreed on how we should plan for the longer-term future of the business. Now that our existing clients were spending more post-credit crunch, Agenda21 was profitable and growing and the extra income would go straight to our profit. With any media campaign, it takes the same effort to do a £750k campaign as it does a £1m campaign but, as we take a percentage as income, we make more money. The year ending 2013 would see us make in the region of £750k profit and because we were not getting distracted by other sideline investments, the profit was ours personally when we wanted it: £250k each.

I believed that digital marketing was not going away and that a business like ours would be in demand for a while. We had carved a niche for ourselves at the more technical end of media and there was nothing to stop us from working with other agencies to deliver a wider range of services.

My view was simple: we have a machine that makes money while we sleep; why on earth would we want to sell it?

Pete and Rhys thought differently. Rhys had viewed the business as a thing with a definite time limit on it and we were eight years in. He wanted to crystallize some value now. Pete was in a different position and I suspect he thought that, despite us being a successful, award-winning company, the company used to have more kudos and profile in the market. I would have taken the profits as dividends for the next few years.

All the books that talk about the importance of shareholder alignment are right, but sometimes life just gets in the way. We had reached the point where we'd spent many years working to build something. Now it was built, we had differing views of what to do with it.

When we sold Media21 to Grey Global, I remember asking Steve Felsher, the CFO, what would happen if he took a dislike to one of us and wanted to get rid of that person. He replied that, in his experience, a far greater concern was the potential for us to fall out – which would put his investment in jeopardy. At the time, that idea seemed absurd, but it now makes sense. It also shows why the £1m profit barrier acts as a stress-test for the leadership team for what lies ahead.

Felsher, at the time, had suggested we read the business book *Built to Last* about the characteristics of great companies. I didn't read it then, but I can now understand what he meant. From his point of view, a business with multiple principles was a risk. One way of de-risking that investment was to have a business that ran regardless of whether the principles left or not.

Whatever our differences, the reality was that, whether we were to sell or not, we needed to continue to build and run the best business we could. Maximizing growth and profits is good for shareholders and will also be reflected positively in any sale. Either way, it's the right thing to do.

Lesson 58: Boost profitability: use the right tools

An initiative I called the Profit Improvement Programme or PIP was transformative. With the PIP, we were able to understand the flow of income and the cost associated with it through the four main areas of the business. Up to then we had a good steer on the company's overall profitability, but we made decisions on resourcing based on what we could see; to be honest, there was an element of gut feel. That meant we were overstaffed in some areas and understaffed in others. The PIP gave us an objective control mechanism.

It was actually quite simple and followed my Golden Rule. Income was allocated to one of our four "product" areas of media, paid search, SEO and analytics. We could match the cost of compensation against each of the four teams and our target was that each team's salary bill could be no more than 50% of income. The remaining 50% was the team's "contribution" to the agency to fund all the other business overheads (rent, equipment, non-billable people like management and finance). As a rule of thumb, it made things straightforward for each team head. If you can't measure it, you can't change it. I was looking for "levers" with which to control the business and found them in the PIP. It worked incredibly well.

Almost overnight, it changed the nature of the conversation in our company. People stopped focusing on how busy they were and how they needed more people and everyone's attention turned to how to be more efficient. It was as if everyone's attention shifted suddenly from one thing (I need more people) to another (I'm going to get the best out of what I've got). Having a proper control mechanism helped us not just to see how much better the business was operating; it also empowered our people to make their own contribution to profitability.

Lesson 59: Ramp up marketing and sales: have clear product pitches and marketing messages – and use them

As well as boosting profitability as we got ready for sale, we wanted to boost sales. We hired a sales and marketing leader called Andy Brown, a rare hunter–farmer hybrid.

In line with the PIP, we began to talk about Agenda21 as having four products, four things that we did really well. Our elevator pitch around forensic analysis was landing well and I was starting to like the idea of naming our products.

Our search engine optimization service became Human SEO, with a focus on SEO being sustainable long term. Forensic Analysis became the working title for our data team's product, reflecting the depth and detail we offered in terms of understanding the drivers of our media work in generating client business. Amplify became our lead in paid search. And, lastly, our media product became Human Algorithm. Programmatic media was really taking off and it was very heavily focused on the technology. Our view was that technology was only one side of the coin. If everyone uses the same technology in the same way, they get the same results, so combining this with smart people makes better results.

Andy also turbocharged our sales effort, doing all the things we were bad at, like following up on leads properly. He helped us refine our pitches, and he brought a lot of value to the business by focusing on the way we communicated with the outside world. Better product differentiation meant that we were better placed to work with larger companies, and to offer our product portfolio more systematically.

We were now in a very competitive marketplace and we were getting better differentiated. Our elevator pitch, a focus on our four key products, better sales and marketing, rinse and repeat. It made the whole operation feel bigger than it really was.

Lesson 60: Build a high-performance team – and be ready to give them the autonomy they need to make a difference

One of the consequences of the PIP was that, to become more self-sufficient, each team needed the right senior management. This was not without its challenges. To motivate and reward our senior managers, we appointed them as legal directors of the company and started a share option scheme.

We also enrolled two of our key people on the Vistage Key Group Programme. The aim was that they would develop and become better able to deal with the day-to-day running of the business. It certainly helped them to get better, but the problem we faced was that, as a leadership, we weren't ready to give up much control. We were focused on building up the company to sell and weren't ready to cede much control or provide the budgets needed for the initiatives they were trying to develop.

The result was – unsurprisingly – that one of these key people left us.

Surrounding yourself with people with complementary skills really does make sense, but you've got to empower them too. We should have been more honest with ourselves that, after spending eight years as a small team of founders, it was going to be harder than we realized to allow others to take control. We were tight-knit and unwilling to give up decision making. We should not have made the commitment to our senior people without being able to see it through.

Being unable to cede control is very common with owner managers, even though the desire to do so – and the understanding that it's necessary – may genuinely be there. It's hard, after building up a way of working, often over many years, to make the change and bring in others. Ironically, though, this is just what many companies need as they approach an exit. They need a succession plan for whoever is going to take the company on in the future. Always have a plan for if and when the founders leave following an exit.

Lesson 61: Getting sale ready – plan ahead and give yourself 12 to 18 months

Media21 was an exception; we sold a company based on its potential rather than its current financial position. We knew we could not rely on such a boom market when it came to Agenda21. Nevertheless, by 2014, Agenda21 was in the best business shape ever. The long slow drag of the credit crunch was behind us, and the idea of a sale began to creep into our thinking. The market was maturing and we were starting to suffer with larger customers by being a smaller independent company and not part of something with a bigger offering.

But we still had time, and decided to give ourselves 12 months to get sale ready. We used this time to focus on the kinds of things outlined in the lessons above: improving our marketing reach; defining our products more clearly; stabilizing our senior team and – crucially – focusing relentlessly on generating profits.

We had also either closed or removed distracting side businesses. Even DataShaka, by far our biggest investment, was running with a separate team so that its time commitment from us was not excessive.

That said, we still felt like a well-kept secret: impressive on the inside but less visible on the outside. In fact, with the exception of our JV partner, Rapp, we had not had much in the way of interest from prospective buyers. While digital marketing was important and growing, many of the larger companies had finally got to grips with it, so our competitive advantage was shrinking. Being better was becoming increasingly difficult to demonstrate. That's why taking the time to plan was so crucial.

Anticipating what buyers would be looking for meant we had time to get ourselves in the best shape we could. It meant that when we did eventually come under scrutiny there would be fewer opportunities for a buyer to beat us down on price.

SELL

Chapter 6

Lessons for selling

Every company sale is different and a huge amount of emotion will likely enter the process here. After all, this is something you may have spent years building; feelings are likely to be strong.

There are many things you can control, like getting your company in the best shape and thinking ahead about potential buyers' concerns and de-risking them. There are also things you cannot control, like the economy. And then there are the curve balls. The crazy left-field things that you could never anticipate – some may be good; others less so.

Deal structures are changing too. Mine have followed a pattern of 100% sale with an initial consideration and an earn-out. Management buy-outs (MBOs) are common and more recently I have been seeing a different type of private equity (PE) deal where they take a minority stake – usually so that the business can invest in further growth, helping it to scale up.

Remember that you will have to live with the post-sale scenario so make sure you know what you are getting into. And remember that doing nothing is always an option. You can only sell once and maybe now is not the right time.

Lesson 62: Timing and the economic cycle: the impact on deal structure

A lower company valuation with a higher earn-out can work well when things are booming early in the economic cycle, although there is always the risk the buyer is trying to acquire you on the cheap with the tantalizing promise of future earnings growth. However, later in the cycle, if recession strikes, the buyer risks demotivating the acquired team with targets they feel unable to reach – arguably through no fault of their own.

A higher valuation and lower earn-out can also work but the risk to the buyer can be high with a demotivated management team who have already made most of their money. The buyer risks spending a lot to acquire a company that could ultimately fail.

In our experience, every potential buyer was serious and also concerned that the potential deal should work. The structure of the deal is often a big factor in whether an acquisition will fail, especially if external circumstances change. When we sold Media21, and the dot-com bubble burst, there was no prospect we would hit our growth and profit targets – not unreasonable given that we sold in a booming market. Getting the deal right, in a way that protects both buyer and seller and also works if the market changes, is tricky. Timing the economic cycle is a major factor to take into account and, as any seasoned investor will tell you, almost impossible to get right.

Lesson 63: Don't let your emotions get in the way of the right deal – focus on the bigger picture and don't fixate on small details

With Media21, our first meeting with a potential buyer started well enough, but it was clear we could not agree on how to value the business. Applying the usual multiple to our non-existent profit did not reflect the potential of the business, the growing dot-com market and the potential value of us to Grey Global's division, Beyond Interactive. Grey's CFO outlined how they usually valued and bought companies, but did it in a way that felt patronizing to me. I was annoyed because, of course, we felt that Media21 was different to all their other acquisitions; we were going to change the world. The impasse threatened to derail the deal.

After much to-ing and fro-ing we eventually agreed an initial consideration payment based on turnover rather than profit with a longer than usual four-year earn-out where we would receive a percentage of additional growth that would be paid at the end of each year. The structure of the deal made our priorities clear: focus on growth for the first two years; focus on profitability for the next two years. All being well, that was.

We learned that it's all too easy to fixate on the small details of an agreement and to lose sight of the bigger picture. Grey's business model was based on their consumption of small, innovative start-ups like ours and there wasn't anything special about us and our company. Naturally, we valued our business more than Grey did and getting the deal over the line required us to understand the other party's motivations and arrive at a good deal that left both parties happy. Or to put it another way, we'd extracted the maximum value we were going to get from a wily old New York ad man.

Hindsight showed it was the right thing to do. We completed our deal in April 2000. The NASDAQ peaked on 10 March and the blue paper was lit for the dot-com crash to come. Sometimes *not* walking away is the right thing to do.

Lesson 64: The right advisor can help you reach the widest audience of potential buyers. Beware doing it yourself

The sale of Media21 was very much an exception; demand was strong and potential buyers sought us out. Most companies will not experience this, and it was true for Agenda21. The first thing we had to do was appoint an advisor to help find buyers and to support us with the sale process. In the advertising business there are a number of companies that specialize in mergers and acquisitions. Our Finance Director and I took on the task of finding the right one so as not to have everyone distracted. Out of several candidates, one said we were too small for them, and a partner at another one was an old flatmate of mine and personally I felt it was too close for comfort, so we chose a company called Results International. They understood us, had worked with companies like us before and we all thought they would bring a lot to the sale process. In particular, they were very well connected in the industry and therefore with prospective buyers.

Was this a process we could have managed ourselves? Possibly yes but, with the best will in the world, we would not have been able to focus and drive the process so well without an advisor. The right specialist help at the right time was crucial.

Lesson 65: Your Investor Memorandum is your shop window. Spend time getting it right; you can only sell your company once

Results International were not going to be cheap; there was a retainer to Agenda21 for a minimum of 12 months and then a percentage on the sale value that the shareholders would have to pay personally. The only upside to this was that the fees would count as part of the sale and would not be subject to tax, reducing our tax bill due from the sale.

During initial conversations we covered the likely process and tactics we could use and possible outcomes. Everything seemed good. The main job was to produce an Investor Memorandum (IM) that summarized Agenda21, the sector we operate in, our financial performance and forecasts and the buying opportunity. Much like an estate agent produces sales collateral for a house, our IM did the same for the business. The IM was anonymous, codenamed Project Hawk, which sounded suitably mysterious to us.

Our investment story was one of growth, specialism and award-winning work driven by a senior team with a proven track record. Our aim of building long-term sustainable relationships with clients was borne out by the fact that we had a number of clients who had remained with us for five, six or even seven years. Our FD was keen to promote the fact that we had recently retained a major customer in a competitive pitch as further evidence of our stability and credibility. We had moved from a company entirely reliant on its founders to one that operated with, but independent from, us. We were mindful of the words of Grey's Steve Felsher all those years earlier, when he'd expressed his concern about the potential for acquired founders to fall out being more of a risk than their companies failing. We recognized the concerns of potential buyers and removed risk wherever we could.

We were in a growing market with stable clients, great profitability and a talented management team. I was especially proud that most of our clients used us for more than one product, meaning we had real capability in a number of areas. We had worked hard to build a story that we could use to create a compelling IM.

Lesson 66: Meet as wide a range of suitors as you can. Demand can come from interesting places you hadn't previously considered

Naïvely, we thought there would be huge demand to buy Agenda21. After all, digital was a core skill still missing from many agencies. We were wrong.

Our interested parties fell into three groups: large agency networks; smaller listed agency networks; and companies that were interesting but less well established.

We thought the larger networks would be the most obvious buyer for Agenda21, partly based on our experience with Media21 and partly because we were familiar to them – we had worked for them before starting up in the first place. The prospect of returning to a network did not fill us with joy. It would be more a question of holding our noses and tolerating an earn-out in a larger company where we would have less autonomy and control.

Of the larger networks none went very far. Despite our long-term partnership, Rapp, part of agency group Omnicom, didn't make an offer. We met WPP and their view was we would not add much they didn't already have. Aegis were the same. It was disheartening to think people were not especially interested in something we had worked so hard at.

We were much more successful with the smaller networks. Both Next15 and Creston (now Unlimited Group) showed a lot of interest. We plugged a gap in their capabilities, and they offered the potential for us to grow and develop by working with a wider group of companies. Our motivation was the same as it had always been: how could we find and win more business and how could we make our existing business more secure by offering a wider range of services to make us "stickier"?

What we hadn't anticipated was that the most interesting demand would come from non-conventional places that, compared to the networks, were quite interesting. It makes sense when you think about it – the indies fitted with our ethos better – but we might not have come across them had we not been working with our advisor.

Lesson 67: Think beyond the deal. Do not ignore the fact that you will be living with what comes after the transaction

The process of meeting potential buyers does begin to focus your mind on what might happen after the sale. It was something we had not really discussed; it was only when we were talking to real-life buyers that it became something real rather than theoretical.

The closest analogy I can think of is when you are expecting your first child. Everything seems to focus on the process of the birth. The idea that you will soon have a baby living in your home gets lost somewhere in the baby books and birthing classes. It was the same with our sale: we were thinking about the transaction and money but not so much about what life would be like afterwards.

However, as owners, it's more than likely that you'll still be involved in the business after any acquisition; it's crucial to think longer term. Some buyers may simply want the founders to stay on for a short time as continuity for customers and staff. For others there is an expectation that the founders will stay on post-deal to run and develop the company they are buying.

In most cases, the day after you complete the sale of your company, you will go back to work. Things might still feel the same, but everything will have changed: you will have a new boss. You need to get this right.

Lesson 68: Don't be afraid to walk away from a bad deal – even if it is from an appealing buyer

With Agenda21, we received a surprising offer from an independent advertising agency group – one that we could not quite believe. It was way below the level we would have expected. The headline offer was a low multiple on our profits, and they wanted to use our balance sheet to pay for part of the deal – the money we had accrued in our business to date. In other words, our own money would be used as part payment for our company. We were surprised, to say the least, as the money had already been earned by the company and therefore belonged to the shareholders. We said that we were interested, but definitely not on those terms.

It became obvious to us that the agency was accustomed to buying companies that were in trouble. Making a low offer and using other assets to part fund the purchase could have been appealing to a company with limited options, drawn to the prospect of working with a bigger company who were growing rapidly and offering much in the way of new business opportunities. However, we weren't in trouble and while the idea of becoming part of the group was compelling, we were not going to sell ourselves short.

Giving up money now for more later is the decision most of us make in setting up a company in the first place. There are companies who have made more money than expected on their earn-out, but from what I've seen, they are the exception. To make that sacrifice twice – once on start-up and then on sale – was not attractive, despite the strategic opportunity that the sale presented. This time, walking away was the right thing to do.

Lesson 69: Pause the whole process if need be. It's emotionally tough but the right deal will come along eventually

When we were selling Agenda21, and had received only a limited number of offers, we still tried to make progress on these regardless of the fact that we were not that excited or inspired by our potential buyers. Strangely, perhaps, the idea of stopping or postponing the sale was simply not an option we took seriously. This kind of process tends to build its own momentum. Once we were underway, we had emotionally switched to a different mindset – one that required a change that would come from being part of something bigger. We had come this far and we were excited by the future; it would have been difficult to call a halt and go back to our day jobs. It made me realize that we had triggered a chain of events that was difficult to stop. I was surprised by the extent to which starting the sale process changed our outlook.

It's crucial, though, that you are prepared to pause the whole process rather than taking the best deal from a bad bunch. Unless you are a distressed seller, having patience and sitting it out for a while can often be the right thing to do. It's emotionally tough, but it's often better to wait for the right deal to come along in the long run.

In the end and out of the blue, a man called Peter Scott sent us an email saying he was interested. Peter had a strong track record in our industry and was setting up a company called Be Heard. His plan was to use this company to buy a number of complementary companies that would offer a range of digital services to advertisers. While the companies would retain their separate operating models, they would be able to co-operate and potentially introduce clients to each other. Be Heard was an interesting buyer that came to us late and would prove to be just the opportunity we were waiting for. Our patience had been rewarded.

Lesson 70: Think about deal structures and securing a premium

In an ideal world, you want your company to be bought rather than sold. What I mean is that, ideally, you want your sale to generate some form of competition between potential buyers that inflates the price of the company. The headline amount that a company will sell for is usually a mixture of two variables. First, the profits of the company, which reflect how big the company has become and will have a multiple applied to them. Competition can boost the multiple paid as buyers compete to acquire the company. And obviously, this is a negotiation. It is subjective and, as with early-stage valuations (see Lesson 14), things like unique technology, a unique proposition or dominant market share can all increase the multiple.

The second key variable is the value associated with keeping a company's founders aligned with the business post-sale. This is especially important where the founders are particularly associated with the business, its customers or products, as was the case with service companies such as Media21 and Agenda21. In this case, a post-sale earn-out is a common mechanism, tying the founders in for a period of time post-sale by offering them ongoing remuneration that shares in the company's future growth.

With Media21, our main challenge was valuing what we were selling and what Grey was buying. Buying companies is common practice in ad agency groups and it is one of their main drivers of growth and innovation. Usually a multiple of between 5 and 10 is applied to the company's net profit (also known as EBIT: earnings before interest and tax) to establish a value. So, a business making £1m profit could be worth £5m to £10m. As we made no profit, we had to agree on another way of valuing our business. And our value was based on a shortage of agencies and a shortage of skills in a booming market.

Unusually, Media21's earn-out was a four-year deal with our payments based on turnover growth for the first two years (if we hit a certain growth target then we would receive a multiple of the turnover figure that was above the target) and based on turnover plus profit for the second two years. If we exceeded a target for both, then we would receive multiples of them. The formula in both cases was a sliding scale rather than a binary hit or miss target: more growth meant a higher multiplier and a higher pay-out. The worst situation to be in would be missing a target by, say, a few pounds and missing out on any payment whatsoever, and I'm sure deals like this have been struck by naïve sellers. Our deal meant that we would get paid for growing the business, with bigger money only associated with higher levels of growth. It was fair and worked for both buyer and seller.

For Agenda21 the headline deal with Be Heard was a six-times multiple based on our net profit with an earn-out that had the potential to pay out the same amount again, provided certain growth and profit targets were achieved.

The experience of selling two businesses in different economic climates and at very different stages of evolution taught me that no one size fits all. It's crucial to think clearly about the structure of the deal and whether it represents a fair deal for both parties.

Lesson 71: The deal that is right for the company may not be right for all the individuals concerned

While the sale to a new buyer should be the best thing for the company and while there is usually an expectation that the founders will continue post-sale, the interests of company and founders may not always align. In my experience, it is rare that a buyer will want to get rid of one of the founders, but that doesn't mean that the founders will want to stay on post-sale.

Very early in our Agenda21 conversations, Be Heard's Peter Scott dropped into the conversation that he had just offered a job to a new CEO. My heart sank. It was not really something I had thought about until he mentioned it but, in the back of my mind, the prospect of taking a wider role in Be Heard was something that had really excited me. I was an unknown to Peter and I recognized I would need to earn the right to the role, but the timings were wrong.

The next day I spoke to Pete and Rhys and said I didn't see a role for myself once the sale had taken place now that a CEO was joining. Looking ahead, I could see a situation where I'd get frustrated with no room to grow into the new company and Pete and Rhys would get frustrated with me being in the way. So, while the continuity of my involvement would be helpful, as a grown-up management team it also made sense that my involvement post-sale should be limited. My salary could be better used to bring in someone else.

Once I had made the decision, my attention shifted to protecting my interests. I did not know Be Heard and my concern was that, once we broke the news that there was no role for me, I could easily be sidelined and disadvantaged during the sale process.

I considered my options carefully and decided that I wanted two things. The first was a clean exit, one that got me out with the full value of my share of the company in cash. I did not want to hold shares in a company I had no impact on and that would probably be illiquid (ie it would be very difficult to sell them). I also wanted to be treated fairly.

What started as a two-way negotiation became a three-way agreement. I had to face the fact and acknowledge that what was in the best interests of Agenda21 was not right for me personally.

Lesson 72: Anticipate due diligence – and prepare for it to be a full-time job when the time comes

Like all acquisitions, the headlines of our deal for Agenda21 were subject to a due diligence process. Although we were a well-run company in terms of having good documentation of things like board meetings, client contracts and company processes, the due diligence was still fairly onerous.

The main focus of a due diligence process is to give the buyer comfort that they are buying what they think they are buying and that there were no nasty surprises. Expectations should be met with the reality that the company is as well run as it appears to be. Once again, this is all about mitigating risk, this time for the buyer in relation to the purchase. Nobody wants to buy a company only to see its major customers and some key people walk out the door the next day.

For Agenda21, we had to provide all the essential paper-work, starting with basics like up-to-date contracts with customers and current employees. Our buyer also wanted to survey our customers to make sure they were happy and not a flight risk. The founders also had to sign a wide range of warranties, including that the company was actually ours to sell and that there was nothing materially important that we had not fully disclosed. Even our other directorships were investigated to ensure that we would be fully focused on running their newly acquired business.

Buyers will be on the look-out for things like unforeseen financial liabilities, such as pension obligations, or outstanding legal challenges and debts – all significant risks to a buyer which should be disclosed.

We had no option but to start at the beginning and to keep going until it was done, posting the information needed on a secure data room platform. Funnily enough, the hardest part of the due diligence process was getting a definitive grip on how many employees we had. At the time we were growing, taking people on and we also had people leaving. Over the weeks of diligence, we repeatedly had to update new starters and leavers.

On the whole, it went well. Our only black mark was that we scored a little patchily on satisfaction feedback from some clients. We could have avoided this if we'd had a formal process for collecting client feedback long before the sale. And not just because of the sale process; it is simply good business practice, especially in a B2B environment. It would have been even better to have had a formal scoring process so we could work to be better, identify detractors earlier and have a better process for dealing with less positive comments.

Ultimately, the best way to anticipate due diligence is to run the best company you can. Don't try to hide anything and identify and resolve any issues before you get to this stage. One company I know had several international offices, each with different ownership structures involving joint-venture partner companies. The structure was too difficult to unpick and it prevented their sale for another two years until they were able to resolve it. This should really have been resolved before going to market.

Lesson 73: Keep lawyers in their place. They can easily derail a deal

Lawyers have an important role to play in any deal, but, in my experience, that can lead to unnecessary complications. I felt, with my plans to exit Agenda21, that my lawyers were trying to achieve something impossible – remove all risk to me from the transaction. In fact, with things getting so convoluted, the legal side of things had the potential to derail the whole deal.

What it boiled down to was a judgement I had to make on whether it was realistic and likely that the buyer would try to get out of their obligation to me once the sale had been completed. My paranoid head said it was possible. My logical head said it was very unlikely that a listed company would behave in such a way; it would send out all the wrong signals to future acquisition targets if they played dirty with their first company. This was where our adviser's wisdom really came into play. He said that it was not possible to plan for every eventuality in legal terms and it was unlikely that the buyer would misbehave. I told my legal team to stop trying to pin down every detail and we got on with the deal in hand.

I learned that lawyers are great at stopping things. Their role is to review the detail of the deal, but I decided that there are times when you just have to accept a risk in order to move things forward. Having a legally watertight structure and no deal would have made me safe but, in the end, there would have been no deal either. In the end, getting out cleanly was surprisingly easy. It turned out that the buyer did not want me as a significant shareholder anyway. I was going to be leaving Agenda21 as soon as the deal went through. They offered to pay me in cash provided I signed a two-year non-compete clause. Ideally, I would have liked this to have been shorter, but I still decided to accept it. In the end, the two years proved too long, but only by about six months. It did prevent me from doing a few jobs post-Agenda21 but I took the view that, on balance, it was a price worth paying. Once again, focusing on the bigger picture helped me to see a way ahead.

Lesson 74: Don't allow a well-meaning buyer to distract you from the job you need to do post-sale

The brilliant book *When Cultures Collide* (by Richard D. Lewis) discusses how to work and communicate across cultures and nationalities. It deals with the ways in which different nationalities conduct business. In particular, I like his insight into the American way of working and how they view the British. Allowing for a degree of national stereotyping, in essence, when it comes to negotiating, Americans lay out their position on the table and then expect to horse-trade. The two parties may argue but it's only business after all. Once agreement is reached, hands are shaken, any bad feeling is left behind and everyone moves on.

The British negotiate in a different way, preferring to hold some items back. A negotiation will move backwards and forwards and during the process additional negotiables will be introduced in order to secure an advantage. With other Brits, this is understood but conflict soon arises when you pit the British against

Americans. To us Brits, it is inconceivable that an American isn't holding something back. To an American, it seems dishonest to reveal hidden items midway through the process.

So, the British see Americans as argumentative horse-traders while the Americans view the British as difficult. Neither position is true but such different approaches offer plenty of opportunities for culture clash.

I fell foul of such a clash after the sale of Media21 when I received a message from our US parent company, Beyond Interactive, asking me to outline our process for entertaining customers. I told them it was not something I had ever really thought about: we entertained customers we liked more than those we liked less, and we spent more on our larger customers than on smaller ones.

My approach was not good enough; they wanted a formal process, something they could harmonize across different countries. They thought I was holding back – being awkward – when in actual fact I simply didn't have the time or inclination to do it.

This was the first of many admin requests that were time consuming and took me away from my real job of running Media21. In the end, I said, "No more."

With such a large potential market at their disposal, US companies often obsess about scalability and tend to focus on company processes that can scale up quickly. In the UK, we have a far smaller market and I viewed scalability as some-thing that would distract from the business of hitting our earn-out targets. It put us on a collision course with our US parent who wanted to make a process out of everything but, in the end, it was the right thing to do – even if they saw us as being difficult.

Lesson 75: Think about what happens to you, as well as the business, post-sale

After 10 years of growing and running Agenda21, the hardest part of the whole process was when I woke up the day after the deal went through and realized that I didn't need to go to work. The fact that the business was continuing without me was stranger still. I felt unceremoniously dumped out of Agenda21; not even two months previously, the idea of me leaving would have seemed absurd. It felt close to a bereavement. I was delighted to have been paid so much money but, equally, I had lost the thing that gave me purpose, fulfilment and status. My next step was to figure out what I should do now.

This is the part nobody seems to talk about and it was especially true in my case, as it was never really part of my plan. And it really was a shock to the system.

Many founders struggle with life post-sale. I did not regret the sale but understandably I was left feeling a lack of direction. What was my purpose in life now?

Professionally, I felt too young to retire and too young to do the non-exec thing so I decided it was time to give something back. I continued with Vistage for another 12 months, paid for out of my own pocket, and I joined a business accelerator to help mentor other start-up businesses and help them to raise finance. My work with DataShaka also continued and I started doing consulting work that would not put me in breach of my non-compete clause.

Looking back, I'm very glad that I didn't rush into anything. I needed the time to reflect on everything that had happened. The sale was the end of a chapter of my life, for sure, but it has also given me an opportunity to open a new chapter. I recommend that any founder/owner thinks ahead when going through a sale process. It might not pan out exactly as you first think, so consider all options and be ready for as many eventualities as possible.

Epilogue

I have realized that I am actually a business man. What I am good at, and what I love, is helping businesses to grow. So, I decided to write it all down – part of my next chapter is this book.

So many people told me they wanted to read my story, but I wanted to do it in a way that would be useful to other people in similar positions. If I had known then what I know now, I would have made many decisions differently – some things I would have done better and many things I would not have done at all.

I've realized that, although I have spent my whole career working in the media industry, what I know is relevant for business more generally. I seem to be good at getting businesses to grow. In fact, the brutal lesson of the dot-com bust has meant I have almost never lost money. In many cases, it is just a case of getting the basics right and this is true for most companies, regardless of whether they are service-based or not.

Sales are critically important; so is cash: a lack of either will easily kill a company.

Getting the right people on board is another obvious win and having poor-performing people can be a huge drag on the business. Hire slowly and fire fast.

De-risking is fundamental too. I often ask myself the question: if I wanted to kill this company what would I do? This helps you to see where the critical risks lie and you can begin to deal with them.

Being able to see the wood for the trees is also a surprisingly elusive quality. I'm amazed at how many leadership teams are so ensconced in their business they cannot see things that are obvious to an outsider. That's why the next step in my career is to help leadership teams and company owners to maximize the value in their companies.

I hope that even if you only learn one thing from this book, it will pay back its cost many times over.

Good luck and stay focused!